MIND
THE GAME CHANGER

DR. R. VISWAKUMAR MD

© **Dr R Viswa Kumar 2022**

All rights reserved

All rights reserved by author. No part of this publication may be reproduced, stored in a retrieval system or transmitted in any form or by any means, electronic, mechanical, photocopying, recording or otherwise, without the prior permission of the author.

Although every precaution has been taken to verify the accuracy of the information contained herein, the author and publisher assume no responsibility for any errors or omissions. No liability is assumed for damages that may result from the use of information contained within.

First Published in April 2022

ISBN: 978-93-5611-006-9

BLUEROSE PUBLISHERS

www.BlueRoseONE.com

info@bluerosepublishers.com

+91 8882 898 898

Cover Design:

Aveek

Typographic Design:

Tanya Raj Upadhyay

Distributed by: BlueRose, Amazon, Flipkart

Contents
of mind are countless, boundary-less

Contents of the book too are not containable in few pages

Every letter is a letter for tomorrow

Every word is the promising word given for a bright future.

Dwell in them well

Experience alone can make you understand, not the explanation.

Introduction

'I think, therefore I'm'...was a philosophical statement by a French philosopher, Rene Descartes. Mind is the proof that you exist, and you are conscious. Human life is synonymous with what you think, such is the mind

Mind, the most fascinating endowment of humans. The mind doesn't seem to have any boundaries...our ability to imagine with no limitations says that. Fraction of a second it takes to relive past or project to future. Plays music with perfect orchestration when music lingers in their mind. Your eyes do not perceive what they see, ears can't perceive what they hear when you are absent-minded. Mind is the sense of all senses and is described as sixth sense even. Memories of the mind are intriguing. Nostalgic experiences are incredible. The intelligent quotient of brilliant minds is enigmatic. Much of the theory, the hypothesis put forth by Einstein has emanated from the mind, rather than physical laboratory experiments.

If there is anything that is least explored by science, that is the mind. The search of science is always outward and it has its limitations to explore the mind because purely science depends on observable, perceivable, measurable, and reproducible physical parameters which do not apply to the mind.

The mind can be explored by the mind only. Each will have to explore the mind on their own to realize its potential. The healing potential of the mind of any disease is grossly ignored, underestimated, and even discarded by modern science, but it speaks of so many psychosomatic disorders nevertheless. The body does what the mind believes in. The function of the mind as a biological clock is unfathomable. The concept of placebo in pharmaceutical and clinical research is not understandable unless we believe in the healing potential of the mind. The mind can create what you believe in. The mind can literally rebuild a mansion from rubbles, can make poor a millionaire, novice a master, and literally a genie that can get you all that you want…faith being magic.

The amazing, alluring potential of mind enthused me to dwell further on this subject and the very purpose of this book is to share my experience with readers and like-minded, to instigate a further inquiry into the mind and kindle interest in this regard for beginners. Psychology and psychiatry are studies of different domains of mind that deal with normal and abnormal functioning of the mind, while here I intend to explore what all possible for the mind and its potential to manifest anything and everything we can think of. Mind is the threshold of metaphysics and quantum physics opening doors to a boundless world of possibilities.

Unless we are aware of the mind with its flooding thoughts, the present moment is constantly flooded away and we miss the very joy of existence. This awareness is brought about by meditation and makes us realize new avenues, facilitates exploring unexplored, and in a way helps take reigns of life into our hands almost completely. Above all, it helps to enjoy the present which is the secret of happiness. Stop saying happiness nowhere…as you get to know it's now here, as you discover happiness within, that's unveiled by meditation. Happiness can never be by the invention, it is always a discovery within, end of the day.

MIND

THE GAME CHANGER…

This is a reminder of mind

***Mind by itself
being mindful about mind
has to keep us reminding
to mind our mind.***

Foreword

One may be content but it is difficult to say if contentment is equivalent to happiness. Contentment could be viewed as culmination and the result of conflict between happiness and unhappiness. Be it so, human mind tries to find out royal road to happiness which may be utopian or myth or simply nonexistent. To exist is a struggle within and without. But, search for the path towards real happiness continues to meet the needs of the body and soul.

Dr Viswakumar makes an attempt to analyze what makes the person to continue to strive toward his own goal. It takes into account the travails of the individual to meet physical, biological and spiritual needs. By a mix of narration and jugglery of words to drive home his point, he makes a great attempt to infuse positive thoughts and hope in the individual. It can be likened to neurolinguistic programming. As each segment of his writing is complete in itself, there is necessarily some repetition. In a way, it may have the effect of reinforcement.

His quest to share his experience for the benefit of others is simply laudable. I wish him all the best in his future endeavours.

12th January, 2022

Dr.M.S.Sridhar
Principal
Apollo Institute of Medical
Sciences and Research
Chittoor

Prologue

I'm the only son of my parents and was an overprotected child. I had no obligation to make my choices because choices are made already by my father. Consequently, I never had the struggle to think over. I even had a conviction that my parents know best what is best for me and was only at the receiving end all the while. Those were the days of my schooling and as I grew further, I noticed some of my friends choosing their options in sports, games, and volunteering in community services, and even optional subjects of their interest. I use to wonder how they make decisions on their own, without consulting their parents, and couldn't decide which is more appropriate, whether deciding on their own choices or seeking advice from parents.

In situations where there were choices before me, I tried to think over and make my choice, but I was doubting myself if I'm right in choice. I was of course topper in the school, nevertheless, I was lagging when I was struck at a point whenever I had to make my choices in many issues. Being good at studies could never help me to make life easier from every other perspective. I wasn't put in a situation in my childhood that could demand decision-making on my own. Right in my school days the first time I felt what my limitation was though being best in academics. When I attempted to make my decisions on my own, I always felt I better consult someone for advice. Practically given the choice I always tried to confine myself to my comfort zone unless it was inevitable to go a step further. Because going further always made me question my mental, physical abilities, and even social skills. A mind that can't think is blunted and growth further is also stunted.

Particularly in Indian society children are taken too much care of, providing financial security beyond their needs. Children provided with too many comforts tend to remain in their comfort zone as far as possible. Children in a way are disabled in developing social skills and deprived to feel the need to be self-reliant. This practice in the long run leaves behind generations who are not so productive in terms of professional and social domains in life...of course, I'm generalizing too much.

Education is not piling up of memory,

but that

which invokes thinking

...Einstein

Perspectives

Introduction v

Foreword ix

Prologue xi

Belief is an expression of the comfort zone 1

Learning is nothing but getting familiarized with
what we do in gradations 5

Comparisontakes you nowhere 8

Conflicts and Common Interests in Human Relation 12

Fear and Anxiety 18

Being cautious is different from being anxious 21

Hope -The Miracle 26

Conclusions and Judgements do not comply with
 facts always 33

Mechanics of Mind 40

A balanced mind acts, a mind with polarities reacts 49

Meditation brings us closest to present 54

Everything that we see around is the translation of our
thought 56

Complaining is habitual, not always situational 57

Mental conflicts make epicenter of stress 60

Mind is on a constant hunt for happiness 63

We go on trying to invent happiness, but it's always a
discovery within 66

Positive thinking is not as easy as advised
  nor it is difficult 67

Living in a moment is different from
living for a moment 72

How we do is joy, not what we do 75

We are best lawyers for our mistakes and best
judges for others mistakes 78

An open mind opens unknown possibilities 80

Mind is a reflection of one's own experiences, while
experience, in turn, is a reflection of mind 84

We do not know what we do not know 87

You are what you seek and you seek what you are 93

Every problem indeed is disguised form
of its own solution 97

The conscious mind is just the tip of an iceberg 102

Basic needs and beyond, humans crave for 110

Contentment is not containment 113

Meditation settles all your agitation 118

Anything that makes you feel insecure is ignorance 129

Acknowledgments 134

Belief is an expression of the comfort zone

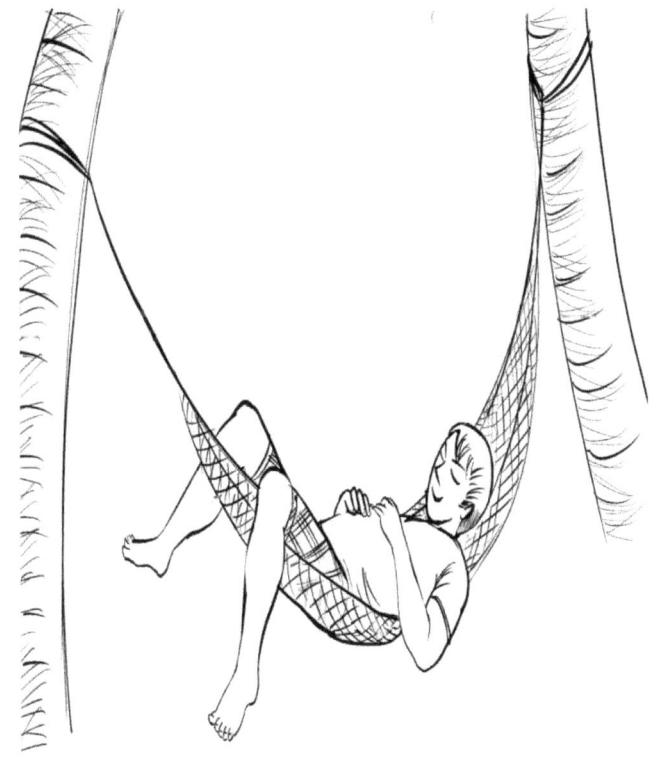

We all live and lead our lives in our comfort zone. Comfort doesn't necessarily mean safe here. But we feel insecure to step out of our comfort zone and continue to endure any attached limitations in the comfort zone, at the cost of progress out of our comfort zone. A false sense of security doesn't let us go beyond. Our beliefs influence us so much that we never bother to check if we are justified in such beliefs. The irony is even when we come to know that our comfort zone is not so safe anymore, still we persist there. Life keeps trying to teach us now and then, to grow beyond our limitations by putting us in a vulnerable state in our comfort zone more often. Either laziness or fear of failure doesn't let us venture anything when we are confronted with testing times.

When a patient visits a doctor and is diagnosed to have some disease, the immediate response of the patient is to ask a doctor if it really warrants any medication or whether he can ignore it. Instead of getting to know what his problem is, he wants to hear from the doctor that he doesn't have to worry about his condition. Suppose if the doctor insists upon some treatment, temporarily he might appear to be giving in but, secretly he wishes to have a second opinion until he finds a doctor who would say or assure that he is not suffering from anything that he needs to worry about.

Similarly, there are many instances in life that make us choose not to believe in what we are confronted with.

When a teacher complains to parent regarding their child's negligence for studies, the immediate response from many parents is to say that his child isn't that sort to be negligent and tries to offer some explanation. This is because he doesn't want to believe that his child is negligent in school. Hardly, in the first instance, no parent is genuinely interested either to listen to what the teacher says or observe himself or herself to know the facts.

A theist doesn't want to believe in atheism. That too in a particular religion, he wants to believe in, he believes. Disbelieves every other religion. *The irony is disbelief in every other religion is part of his belief in his religion.*

All this boils down to belief, which is our secured territory, rather a cocoon we live in. Believing in what you choose to believe is parallelly making you not believe in any other despite proof against belief. This is a highly vulnerable condition that can end up subsequently ranging from simple anxiety to depression, inability to adapt to what is expected to adapt. Failure in a career for many is simply because they believe in their comfort zone. *Conditioned mind in a comfort zonein simplest terms is past impressions costing the future.* Beliefs and comfort zone make our growth stagnant. They do not allow to explore further, be it in life or be it for truth. Comfort zone at the most can help for existence, but never to evolve. At times even existence becomes questionable if we are too resistant to any further changes we need to adapt. Over protected children are brought up in comfort zone. Hardly ever such children feel the need to think of anything further and it seriously disables them when there is imminent need to adapt to something they are not used to. This might sound like too generalized statement. But atleast as far my observation concerned, children grown in bit adverse conditions financially have a sort of killing instinct to fight out their adversity for growing into prosperity. It is really a walk on rope for parents to balance between comforts they can give their children and need to make them realize what the needs and wants are and make them recognize their strength and limitations.

Happiness

We are happy conditionally only when something happens as per our expectations

Learning is nothing but getting familiarized with what we do in gradations

Me being a doctor and professor in a medical institution, my profession constantly demands honing my skills in teaching my students and treating my patients. We need to keep abreast with the latest advances, failing which we will be stagnant and our skill or knowledge could be obsolete over a period of time.

I'm reminded of a funny incident in past. I had been to Chennai to give a screening test for selection into medicine with my friends. Once after finishing while returning we reached the railway station and at the inquiry counter we had to enquire which is the train we should board to reach our home town and when does it arrive. Due to the language barrier, I had to make my inquiry in English and I was rehearsing over and over again before I could speak at the counter as I was being pushed by the crowd behind me at one end. Finally, of course, I made it but I do not remember how appropriate was my inquiry in English. I had my schooling entirely in regional language and there was never a need nor opportunity to catch up with English till I passed out. How our ignorance is a liability we never get to know unless we are thrust upon to acquire the required skill or knowledge. We tend to postpone as much as possible about learning anything new. When learning is optional we are all the more ready to give up, but when it becomes an absolute need or choice, then it takes its toll in all possible ways. This is a well-known fact to all of us but equally ignored or overlooked.

When we think of learning something new, or when there is an absolute need to learn something which we have been avoiding for long, we feel stressed in taking up to learn because at the outset, we compare ourselves with those who have mastered it. For instance, skills like driving a vehicle or computer skills or any such skills that are essential as part of personal, professional or social life (I'm not referring to fine art skills like singing, dancing, painting or playing musical instruments, because these things we choose to learn on our own and we are ready to give what it takes to learn). Before even we start learning, we compare with those who mastered and feel that we stand nowhere before them and give up even, thinking that that's not our cup of tea. But in principle, any skill is nothing more than getting used to it, which means nothing but practice. There is nothing like a prequalification to learn these things. You qualify yourself as you learn with consistent practice. One wonderful quote by martial arts guru Bruce Lee is, he says…' I don't fear a man who learned 1000 ways of kicking, but I fear the one who practiced that one kick for 1000 times…' such is the power of practice. While we are about to learn a skill, the first thing we need to keep in mind is not to compare ourselves with those who mastered it. With one brick in hand, you need not wonder how you can build such a huge wall. Remember we are adding bricks one after the other however big the structure may be.

This applies to students in their studies. They shouldn't think of toppers in their batch while they start studying oreven employees while learning professional skills. One must mind that the practice and skill of anyone around are immaterial to us, whoever it is or whatever skill it is we are contemplating. To climb a mountain when we look at its peak we can't put even one step ahead. We just need to mind going step by step that eventually takes us to the top of the hill. Any target must be divided into small steps and we need to go one step at a time.

The process of learning is very interesting. To start with we are too conscious about how we are picking up. All our hesitancy and fumbling are because we are too conscious and as we consistently practice regularly and over a period of time, there is a shift of this awareness from a conscious level to a subconscious level. We can notice this, for instance in driving a four-wheeler, how conscious we would be about applying break, accelerating, or engaging a gear while learning and how subconsciously we do the same thing after mastering it. So, it is not the ability to learn that matters but, it is always the consistency of practice that brings this awareness from conscious level to subconscious level. Here again, the need to learn or desire to learn can make a difference in the attitude of learning again.

Learning is conscious to start with, then registered and operated from the subconscious mind. Meditation is exactly the opposite of this process. It is bringing the subconscious mind to a conscious level in gradations, so that influence of the subconscious mind ceases over a period, which is essentially unlearning.

Comparison takes you nowhere

We can't expect fish to fly like a bird or a bird to swim like a fish. Each of us has our place, pace, and timeline in life and no two are comparable in any domain. It is almost impulsive for us to keep comparing one with the other. I keep advising my students always to give their best but never use to compare anyone with others. Sometimes we are destined for far more glorious success than what is in the vicinity, outshining even those with whom we compare usually. I can share my own success story in this regard. First time when I appeared for the test for selection into medical graduation, I couldn't even score qualifying marks (was not in the race altogether, leave alone selection). Though I was aspiring and ambitious for studying medicine I never put in enough effort out of sheer negligence. If I were to compare myself with those who succeeded in their efforts I wouldn't have even ventured an attempt further. Subsequent year I prepared with undivided attention and was single-minded all through until I made it. I did it so well that I stood in second place at the state level in the screening test for selection. The success of such magnitude was unthinkable even for me or even my friends at the beginning of my preparation. All that I did is I got completely engrossed in my preparation without even assessing possible outcomes and never bothered to compare myself with anyone else. All in the mind.

Under no circumstances comparison is relevant. It's an absurdity prevailing in all our minds. I go the extra mile to say that, you can't even compare yourself with yourself, thinking how you have been in past and how you are today, leave alone comparing with others. Compared with others is suicidal. Your success in the past might encourage you while your failure from the past can equally discourage you. We may be destined to accomplish more than what anyone around has achieved or more than what we achieved in past. By any standards, the comparison doesn't help in any way. We confine to our comfort zone largely because of these comparisons from the past and with others around us. However old you are, however senior you are...it's never too late to acquire any skill. Another reason for not being able to step out of their comfort zone or to learn something new is... *people never change when the option is given, but they only change when there is no option, but to change.*

Anger

Anger is predominantly shown in a helpless state. Those reactive, show anger while those who are proactive have the right approach for resolving the issues

Conflicts and Common Interests in Human Relation

Following narration is my attempt to explain how relation among people is influenced by various factors at different levels of their needs and wants that creep into relation. Relation just for the joy of it is seldom found even among friends at times. We are all psychologically tuned for competition rather than cooperation. Fundamentally we are ignorant about the fact that we tend to compete only when we feel insecure. This may sound ironic but it's true. Rivalry among siblings, among friends, and heated exchanges between couples, each of these have different reasons that creep into relation at different levels. Cause for conflicts or disputes range from needs to wants and even issues concerning ego and or freedom

Every individual is comparable to a circle. In this circle, at the center, the core is made up of desire for needs and passion for wants. The core is made up of desire and drives for biological needs like food, sex, and sleep. Food in this context refers to livelihood, sex in the context of one's sex partner and his possessiveness and sleep refers to one's shelter or home and comforts. As we go from the center of the circle to the periphery, we see varied inclinations, varied interests and are specific for the individual.

When two individuals get to know each other and as they befriend each other, the interaction at the beginning is at the periphery and conflicts are less likely due to varied interests and relationships will be at the level of no conflict zone. There will be no room for enmity because two individuals in the relation, assuming each as a circle, overlapping of the circle will be minimal. But, when two individuals interact, with some common interests at the peripheral zone, they find comfort in each other's company and start befriending. Common interests like music, sports, or philosophy are at the periphery and common interests at this level bring people closer indeed gradually (assuming each personality of the individual as a circle). If there are no common interests, at the most, they may not befriend and interaction will be formal and non-contradictory. As the relation and interaction deepen further encroaching the core (center of the circle) they encroach on each other upon universally common interests at the core namely food, sex, and shelter.

I'm referring to livelihood when I say food in this context. However best the friends maybe, once they get into financial and commercial entrepreneurship, they end up being enemies, the bottom-line being the security of their livelihood. I'm referring to life partner when I say sex in this context, even the best friends when interested in the same person it leads to rivalry because choosing the partner is something that arises out of the basic instinct to choosing the mate for their progeny which is of course driven by sex. Next to these basic or biological needs of food and sex, arises the need for shelter which can flare up the differences among siblings fighting for their share in whatever assets they are entitled to. Of course, the wealth and assets we struggle to possess are to take care of all these basic needs, comforts, and luxuries and even for an esteemed image in society taking pride in these possessions.

What is more interesting is, however best maybe relation between two persons, issues involving above needs can flare up disputes as mentioned above, but there is something beyond these, for which there is a constant battle for anybody within and without. This battle that goes on and on is a desire for freedom.

Concerning the above needs I mentioned in the foregoing lines...rivalry between two men for the same woman whom they are interested in is understandable. Even if one of these two succeeds in winning the woman he fights for, once they are together on being wedded, even these two partners though they mutually help each other to cater to their basic needs like food and sex, sooner or later they pick quarrels now and then, which might not need a quarrel indeed. Then why though everyother need is met with like shelter, food, and sex, what else bother people in relations...? Even children born in rich families, even elders having amassed huge wealth find some emptiness in their life. We all crave for freedom that we are unknowingly losing in the name of education, culture, and conforming to set standards, be it anything that is designed by society. Freedom is an absolute need everyone is craving for...freedom from being questioned, freedom to be what they are, freedom from poverty (hence the struggle for basic needs). Self-centered thinking, attention-seeking, mutual expectations, identity crisis are also predominantly the source of stress in human relations. True freedom begins when we realize how we are clinging to all above virtues, and when we learn to grow beyond these. Freedom is growing beyond these false perceptions. Nature is inherently designed with a mutual dependency, and mutually complementary traits among the species (interspecies and intraspecies mutual dependency). Even if honey bees become extinct, sooner or later humans will be extinct too...nature is laced with so much interdependency in terms of existence and survival. But hardly humans realize this. A given species is at least naturally inclined to its protection against all the adversity it encounters. But when it comes to humans, all our thoughts and deeds are never in the interest of the human species, but individualized and self-centered. This is a self-destructive right from the individual level to the human species level. We are yet to learn to live together, coexist, cooperate, and adapt to the 'live and let live policy.

The bottom line is the interaction between any two, so long it is confined to the periphery of their individual circle, they can get along well. But as it proceeds towards the core of the circle it encroaches upon fundamental needs…particularly the freedom which the human mind is in search of, beyond food, sex, and shelter, sustainability of relation is questionable and becomes vulnerable. At root level the problem in human relations, to put it simply, I say ' we all think of our rights and others' responsibilities, which is always conflicting…rather we should think of our responsibility and others rights', that never brings any confrontation. When you recognize your responsibility, instantly your rights are entitled, not otherwise. To my surprise after I finished writing these lines, I happened to come across 'levels of needs' described as Maslow's hierarchy of needs as under, that was very similar to my narration in foregone lines. This hierarchy of needs was described under these headings:

Self-actualization

Esteem

Love and belonging

Safety

Physiological

Physiological needs include food, water, sleep, and shelter
Safety needs include employment, morality, and bodily care
Love and belonging include family, friendship, and romance
Esteem needs include respect, achievement, and self-esteem
Self-actualization needs include self-realization and introspection

Among these needs as depicted above physiological needs are at the bottom, which is like the biological needs of any living being and as we go above needs are at the higher plane rather higher mental plane.

Joy

Joy is a higher state than being happy and one can be joyful unconditionally like a kid, an artist involved in the performance. Likewise when we do things just for the joy of it with no expectations.

Fear and Anxiety

When you are chased by a stray dog, flight or fight hormones released in the body, pumping more blood with galloping heart, to fight it out or to flee to atleast from the site of danger. Either way, it is preparing us mentally and physically to survive. But on the other hand same fear, when it is overwhelming, neither it helps to fight nor it gives strength even to flee. It incapacitates most of the time rather. Our reaction in the form of fear or anxiety in a vulnerable state is to be understood in good spirit.

Any living being is destined to survive, grow and evolve. The instinct to survive is deep-rooted and strongest of all instincts. Survival of an individual is by procuring food and survival of species is by reproduction (rather sex), which is why hunger and sex drive are such driving forces. Fear and anxiety are exaggerated in humans due to imagination. Animals when confronted with a threat or when they sense threat lurking in the corner, then they act instinctively out of their fear to fight or flee from the danger, while in humans worry and anxiety is more of their imagination of possible or even unlikely consequences. The extent of anxiety, worry, or stress variable from individual to individual because of their different life experiences and even different levels of imagination. It is not merely about survival in humans, goes beyond worrying about health, wealth, issues concerning status, ego, and boundless often. Reacting to a condition is highly personal and individualized for the same issues confronted by many. Consequently, reaction to the problem largely constitutes the problem. For instance, minor health issues like hyperacidity can incapacitate some, while those suffering from malignancy at times may well accept their condition without allowing the influence of their illness in leading their life as long as they survive.

Acceptance of the problem and prevailing conditions is the first step to check the severity of the reaction. More the unacceptance, more severe the reaction. Unacceptance is largely because of self-centered thinking largely and a sort of self-pity or even ego may make us not accept the given conditions or the problem we are confronted with. Unless we start accepting, we do not go ahead genuinely to deal with it, the way we should. Acceptance isn't a failure, rather the first step is to understand the cause, consequence, and solution of the problem. This attitude of acceptance helps in both ways like it lets you deal with the problem more pragmatically and even check the accompanying anxiety or worry that sets to some extent. Thinking faculty is an ability, humans are endowed with but, we cultivate this into our disability because of overthinking and some psychological factors as mentioned earlier. I do not say no problem is a problem, but would rather say approach and attitude towards problem makes all the difference.

We need to understand that fear or anxiety is a natural reaction intended actually for preparing ourselves, by all means, to 'deal with it' indeed. Most of the time fear or anxiety which is a mental reaction for preparedness to deal with the problem turns out to be a major limiting factor for handling the situation. In all probabilities, the outcome of a situation depends on how well we understand the nature, cause, and consequence of the problem we are confronted with, instead of simply worrying about the consequence. In a way, difficulties we are confronted with are indeed opportunities to grow beyond our limitations. As the saying goes *a ship is safe on shore, but that's not where it is supposed to be.*

Being cautious is different from being anxious

Being tense is being alert. Alertness and readiness in taking up a task ahead. This alertness when overwhelming turns into anxiety. What is meant for defense turns into something disabling us. But in any case, striking a balance between two polarities is always desirable. Being too careless taking things for granted, or being too cautious that turns into anxiety, both are unwelcoming. Most often fear of failure by itself is the cause for failure. Being obsessed with success is the root cause of fear of failure and anxiety. Being ridiculed by others for failure in many issues is the reason for worrying though not exactly the failure that could bother.

Let's learn to stop accepting definitions of success and failure given by society and dancing to its tunes. It doesn't mean always you have to reject norms defined by society. We need to be more discretionary. Other than problems concerning our basic needs and health issues, worrying is optional in many of the issues. Worrying is a misuse of our imagination. All said and done we are the best judges for our problems. You alone can have deep insight into your problem. Probably options available as the solution may not be all that palatable at times and we need to come to terms with realities genuinely sometimes to arrive at a solution. Acceptance of given conditions is the first step for soothing the mind that allows further thinking towards a solution. As I said earlier self-pity or ego comes in the way of accepting things as they are, which makes things more complex to deal with. Sometimes problems are not to be solved, but to be dissolved in course of time on their left alone. because the more we meddle in some situations more it gets complicated. Not necessarily we need to take active steps at solving a problem in some situations. For instance quarrels between couples and even friends when interfered with by others make them more complicated and if left alone might be dissolved in time. Even trivia like roadrage in a traffic jam serves nothing except picking more quarrels. Children sometimes left alone can study on their own in a much better way than when interfered with by parents too often. The majority of arguments are for argument's sake, but never at identifying a solution. When something goes wrong most of the time we are more interested to know who has gone wrong, rather than how and why things went wrong

Acceptance is different from compromise. Compromising is in a negative sense to accepting in a helpless state and surrendering to the situation. While acceptance I'm talking about is,to take stock of the situation, without identifying yourself in the problem, accepting the realities, we formulate a strategy to get out of the problem. In simple terms a positive approach. In Chinese, there is a saying that says… 'one step backward sometimes is only to have two steps forward later. Even an arrow is pulled back before it can be shot fiercely. This is what I mean by acceptance, which is not in a negative sense.

Suppose you are betrayed by your close friend in some issue, not being able to digest this, feeling sorry for yourself for trusting your friend, cursing your fate, and doing nothing is a compromise. Acceptance is understanding that you were gullible enough to be betrayed by a friend and treating it as a lesson and not to repose faith in anybody blindly,you chalk out a strategy for damage repair. It is easier said than done of course. But if you are compromising you are allowing the suffering to continue, but when you accept and act, it is bouncing back after fall. When a stray dog bites, you can't bite it back showing your anger!!(I don't mean this, I mean our reactions could be as silly as this at times losing our discretion) Reactions are mostly because we can't accept things as they are. All that you need to do when bitten by a dog is to rush to the hospital for treatment in time.

Any emotional reaction I mean is natural, but should be momentary and shouldn't blind us to the future course of action. Compromise is a kind of negative approach with a giving up attitude. Acceptance is a kind of coming to terms with realities and being proactive in a given condition. My experience in past taught me that acceptance reduces reaction and over a period of time, there is a shift of mind from reactive phase to proactive phase. Acceptance in the sense, understanding the conditions leading to present condition and realizing that nothing happens without a sufficient cause. This also reduces emotional pain further.

As I said earlier when fortune strikes we never say…why me? But when misfortune strikes we always question why me? Which is the very reason for emotion and reaction. If the reactions of the mind are negated they turn into a response of the mind in a given situation with the right perception. Our reactions are part of our response and a reminder of our responsibility while dealing with some confrontations. One of my close friends keeps telling me often 'it is impossible to be cautious enough however cautious you are.

There are occasions when many teetotalers fell victim to cardiac problems, many studious students have failed and sincerely loving partners have been betrayed…all in the game. There are countless such examples. But unless we take responsibility for what we are we can never go further. Blame a million…but all those complaints are futile and serve no purpose. Remember everyone is self-centered in their thinking, however selfless they may appear. Selfishness varies only in degrees.

Envy

Envy is a sign of weakness. It's the play of mind for mental comfort by not acknowledging the success of others. One who is only focused on the job at hand has neither time nor attention for what is being done by others.

Hope -The Miracle

It is not uncommon to find so-called backbenchers in our group flourishing well in their career surprisingly and so-called toppers in batch, we might not find them as successful as expected at times. One thing we need to keep in my mind always is...*hope is different from expectation, expectations disappoint quite often, but hope never does.* Toppers in the batch may have too high expectations of themselves, while backbenchers thrive on hope. Maybe I'm generalizing too much, I do agree. One of my juniors when I was studying medicine, use to be too good in academics...has abruptly ended his life by committing suicide, the reason being he couldn't bag the gold medal in the examination. Neither backbencher nor topper is my interest here to talk about. What I mean to suggest is *hope, but don't expect...* Some who excel academically may be so injudicious in their approach towards life. Academic success or even success defined by society need not be a success in the true sense always. For me the definition of success is individualized., can't be generalized. *Adopting is a success, to be able to be happy is a success, to be able to enjoy the present is a success.* Waiting to be happy after being rich or famous or accomplishments is a colossal waste of life. Proving yourself to others is futile and is of no consequence. Hope always keeps the doors open. Expectations are bound to disappoint sooner or later. *Hope is work-oriented and expectation is result-oriented.* Neither your failure nor the success of your rival can be a reason to lose hope.

It is our past experiences, the influence of people around, that leave some impressions that create boundaries in our thinking. These impressions only end up creating some limitations. The scope of thinking also narrows down, makes us believe in possibilities only known to us within the confines of our own experience and beliefs. Consequently, we tend to not believe in possibilities that we are unaware of. Due to limitation of previous whatever little experience and preexisting impressions we tend to lose hope in many situations when confronted with problems...mainly because *we don't know what we don't know* and our judgments are only according to whatever little knowledge we have. The problem with half knowledge is that it makes us believe that we know everything and out of this ego that blinds our discretion we tend to rush to conclusions more often than not. We will either be overconfident or more frequently maybe even, we will be hopeless, giving up hope easily, thinking that we know how all solution of the given problem is not possible due to narrow scope of thinking. Concomitantly we give up even attempts at solving the problem.

Contrary to the above scenario let's imagine someone well aware of his ignorance (contrary to one who is egoistic with his half knowledge). He will be humble enough to sense 'what he doesn't know and realize how little he knows he only believes in doing his part, doing his bit when confronted with a problem, and leaves the rest pinning his hopes on God for divine intervention from some unknown quarters.

Suppose if there two students giving their exam,one with lack of hope due to inadequate preparation may abstain from attending exam while other one resting his hopes on god when gives his exam he might as well pass the exam, because the questions that appeared might be well within the purview of whatever little he prepared. The same opportunity is missed by his friend just because he gives up hope.

I happened to receive once a call letter for an interview for placement as faculty in one of the prestigious medical institutes, which is my dream, working as faculty there. But due to heavy competition I wasn't hopeful at all about my selection, nevertheless made it to the interview as scheduled. To my surprise, I was the only candidate to attend and there was no other competitor for me on the day of the interview. As it was raining heavily many couldn't make it to the interview and almost every other candidate applied seems to have dropped. I was the only one to attend and obvious choice too for selection. If I did not attend the interview giving up hopes I would have deprived myself of this opportunity with my own hands.

Giving up hope is never wise, maybe, so-called intelligent may be assessing various possibilities and might give up hope thinking that it is foolish to be hopeful beyond the hope in a given issue. But when wisdom prevails, you believe in divine intervention from unknown quarters and our humble approach paves the way to success in many more ways than we can imagine. *I do not mean nevertheless to hope for impractical unrealistic dreams coming true.*

Long ago I remember it was in the 80s, it was the season for the Sharjah cup series cricket tournament and the final match was between India and Pakistan. We can imagine how heated the moments would be. I vividly remember last over was being bowled by Chethansarma and Miandad was at the strikers' end. The last over was melting away one ball after another, but Pakisthan players were well restricted by Indian players by effective bowling and fielding. The last ball remained to be bowled and the opponent's team needed four more runs to win. The last ball bowled was flung into sixer by a mighty shot by Miandad that fetched them the trophy. This is one perfect example I witnessed that taught me…giving up hope is never wise however hard testing times might look.

On a few occasions the diseases said to be incurable and given up by doctors, have resolved on their own.For instance, some malignancies were reported to have resolved which is simply described as spontaneous resolution. In such cases, if patients were to lose hope resorting to drastic steps like committing suicide, just because it was declared as incurable, can't imagine what it could cost.

Preaching of lord Krishna in Gita speaks of this philosophy that says, our job is only to do our part (duty) and leave the outcome to the will of God, which is aptly described as karma yoga. This is the highest form of philosophy though sounds simple. Clinging to result, spoils the effort.

Past in my life has taught me that, *hoping beyond hope is far more fetching than giving up hope, however hopeless it might look.* Most of the time our overthinking only leads to imagining more and more complex consequences of an existing condition rather than offering any hope. All said and done hope and enthusiasm are two wheels of life. There is no enthusiasm without hope, and life is lifeless without hope or enthusiasm. The concept of benefit of the doubt is merely based on hope. Being hopeful can be transliterated as simply 'allowing possibilities unknown to us'.

Thoughts rob away present

Mind is described by many as simply a flow of thoughts. Incessant, relentless, tireless thinking is what we are indulged in, day in and day out without our consent or being conscious about it.

This relentless thinking can

*Dissipate energies

*Blind the truth

*Obscure the present

*Make us indulge in memory of past and imagination of future

*Make us mistake our thoughts as facts, thereby misleading our direction of approach in a given situation

* leave us dying before we live

Ideas have destiny while thoughts are of no consequence. I'm perplexed and baffled sensing how taxing it is really to be involved in thinking relentlessly. On top of it, whole thinking is irrelevant, doesn't make sense most of the times. Much of this thinking is by auto-piloting, auto play, replay emerging from the subconscious mind that we are unmindful of. Probably an attempt by the mind to organize its database to learn lessons by regret from the past, trying to lay a path for future course of action, but all of it looks so jumbled that we can't make out anything out of any of these thoughts. *The colossal waste of time in our life is not exactly by doing useless things, but because of this clutter in mind with purposeless thoughts.* The brighter side of the picture is, it is our constant quest for happiness. The reason why even such a constant quest is not bringing happiness is that we believe in 'becoming' rather than 'being' happy. When a thought arises in the mind we get carried away by that by responding to it, in turn, our response to thought by itself spurs up another thought leading to perpetual endless thoughts, much like monkeys jumping from one branch of the tree to another. Hence aptly described as monkey thoughts. We need to pay attention and be observant and vigilant about these thoughts, without responding to them. Be a witness or spectator to these thoughts without you identifying yourself in a scenario pertaining to these thoughts. This practice over a period of time cuts down the frequency and intensity of these thoughts, which cease to trouble us gradually.

Another aspect to watch is to pay attention to the nature of these thoughts, I mean what these thoughts are about. This helps you to understand yourself as to what is bothering you. With keen observation, we get to know that no thought is without a reason however absurd it might look. Every thought emanates from deep-seated feelings and emotions about pain or pleasure of physical or mental experience that we had in past more often. Thoughts projected to the future also revolve around 'how happy you can be or you will be' with reference to present condition. As I said, there is one common factor on which, each of these thoughts is woven around. It tries to recollect happy times we had in past, fun that we missed in past, hoping for happy times ahead in days to come, despair when the future is seemingly hopeless for not finding happiness...*everything boils down to happiness. But paradox in life is, planning to be happy is a big hurdle for being happy.* Because according to us happiness is always conditional, dependent on some relation, or acquisition or possession or some achievement or accomplishment. Thoughts keep haunting us until we meet these conditions which we impose on ourselves in search of happiness. *No success or no wealth or no person can confer lasting happiness in our lives.* We being ignorant of this truth keep trying to meet these conditions and our relentless thoughts are part of our attempts at being happy, rather becoming happy. More you understand the futility of these worldly possessions to make us happy, less will be your struggle for happiness, lesser will be troubling thoughts as well. This is not about renunciation I'm talking about, but the realization, that can keep us happy unconditionally. A kid is unconditionally happy because no thoughts trouble it by making it to think of doing something to be happy or be something to be happy.

Conclusions and Judgements do not comply with facts always

We are very impulsive to judge or rush to conclude all that we see, all that we hear, or even all that we think which is more often than not, disastrous or misperception atleast. One fundamental principle we need to keep in mind is, we have no obligation to opine all that we come across. The mind tends to quickly analyze our inputs (what we see, hear or even think) and decipher something or other to decide our stand or approach towards it. Its natural means we adapted to adapt to given conditions. In all fairness when we think, it is our way of learning through our perceptions. But our vision is so colored due to past impressions, our predilection to some presumptions, our ego, insecure feelings all these things do not let us see the things as they are but perceived as we are rather. This may indeed deprive us of a genuine relation, an ideal opportunity, what not anything it might cost as the case may be. We need not be in a hurry to conclude anything as there is no time frame to perceive and opine so quickly most of the time.

A not so well-dressed teacher may be subjected to mockery by students, a junior in working place is considered not to be so competent. The success of others we tend to comment that it's not a big deal or by fluke, whereas we speak so highly of our success. Sometimes we overestimate our abilities or even underestimate them. The list is endless, from the moment we getup from bed, till the time we go to bed, all that we come across, unceasingly we keep judging.

'Don't judge a book by its cover' is a popular quote to remind us of this. Our thinking ability is meant to analyze, not to opine, but because thinking is difficult we rush to opine. More often than not our unwillingness to think is the reason driving us to opine rather than difficulty in thinking. If we are constantly aware that we are the losers more often by opining, probably we might check this habit of opining. Anything that is not compliant with our expectation we tend to opine it bad. These impressions narrow our scope of thinking.

It doesn't always mean that we can't consider the past experience in assessing problems we are confronted with. When past experience enables us to resolve an issue that's well and good. But with your inadequate past experience when you decide to give upon something ...it's better to be hopeful believing in possibilities unknown to you. Giving up hope is like giving up life. As I quoted earlier ' *lifeperishes in pessimism, but not in poverty and flourishes in optimism, not by possessions.* However illogical it might look, still it is not wise to give up hope, because as I said earlier 'we don't know what we don't know.

It is habitual for us to form an impression, and adapt to it, which is essentially a way of learning. What we come across afresh, we extrapolate to pre-existing similar impressions and experiences and start labeling as good, bad following past impressions. This is how the mind got used to processing information to build upon pre-existing data. But essentially we need to unlearn this habit of opining and need to see things as they are. This unlearning needs a very conscious effort, *because opining occurs at a subconscious level almost instantly.* So it needs a conscious effort to curtail this habit of opining instantly. This needs an open mind, serenity to accept things that are probably not possible for an ordinary mind. The plane of thinking is to be elevated. Broader and deeper we need to think, which is made possible only for one who meditates. Meditation is essentially unlearning of an established pattern of thinking or action and deconditioning of the mind. We evolve to the extent of seeing things as they are instead of seeing them as we are. We grow beyond perspectives. Lateral thinking admits observing things, rather than opining. The hardest thing in our daily routine is not to opine. We have our own opinions about right from neighbors to the president and prime minister, regardless of our knowledge of truth in it. Opinions are subconsciously formed as an add-on to preexisting impressions, which may or may not be true. It is essential to guard ourselves against our own opinions as they are not always true. Much of our negative thinking on any issue presented to us is because of our habitual opining almost instantly about almost anything. We keep blaming pollution being unmindful of doing our bit towards it, blame the road traffic though most of the time we violate traffic norms, blame the weather, blame the leaders, blame employer and employees, keep blaming anything insight which is exhausting and energy dissipating, dampening our spirit. All this toll we pay because we tend to opine. This dampens our spirit more than actual prevailing conditions. Meditation facilitates an escape from this hard shell of complaining or opining. Makes us more pragmatic, optimistic paves way for a more productive life, as all that we complain of is a reflection of all that is there in mind. Negative thinking or even expectations both are unwanted and unwarranted. One can be hopeful which is essential indeed. Negative thinking and over-expectation create polarities in the mind that can influence our approach towards the task at hand. But being hopeful and carrying out the task, giving our best brings out the best. *We are so prejudiced that we are the best lawyers for our mistakes and best judge for mistakes committed by others.* At times it is so frightening to realize how prejudiced we are and how colored our vision is. Hardly we ever attempt to validate our opinions. One of my friends keeps telling me often when I'm confused, 'be aware of facts' and try not to rush to conclusions as much as possible. *An open mind opens unknown possibilities while the concluding mind curtails possibilities.*

Misunderstanding is a liability for one who misunderstands but not for one who is misunderstood in our relations be it in family or working place or in any other context. The commonest cause for the wide communication gap amongst us is, everyone thinks that another one is also thinking the same way in a given issue concerned. For instance, one who intends to borrow from a friend thinks that his friend is comfortable enough and willing to lend, though he is not exactly aware of what is in his friend's mind. A teacher thinks that the lesson he is teaching is an easy one to pick, while the student is breaking his head to get to know what it is. A husband coming home late from work once in a while thinks that his wife will take it right sense, while the wife is furious at home waiting for her husband to bang sooner he comes. Every thought, opinion or presumption is ones own perspective.

Instincts are natural, intelligence is mental fabrication and wisdom is to recognize both

Instincts are inborn and never misleading, like a mother's instinct. Mother knows best what child need seven when a child can't speak. Intelligence is an asset only to some extent. Beyond the needs, intelligence makes thinking more complex. In a true sense, wisdom is beyond this complexity of overthinking due to intelligence. Even in our body cells divide in a regular pattern for growth, development, and repair of tissues. But when it is unwanted, uncontrolled cell division, we call it cancer. Similarly, intelligence beyond our needs is like mental malignancy and only distorts, because too many possibilities and consequences are imagined by an intelligent mind before taking up something. Intelligence when matured should culminate in wisdom. Till such time we take pride in our intelligence until proved otherwise. The majority of individuals suffering from depression are because of their high IQ that makes them imagine even the most unusual and unlikely consequences of a situation. Average intelligence is a blessing indeed. Those with average intelligence simply focus on the job in their hand without indulging in much thinking. When intelligence reaches its zenith when it matures into wisdom, we realize how complex this thinking is and our wisdom humbles us leading to the realization that 'what we know is a speck in the ocean'. Those with high intelligence suffer stress for the same reason but when it matures into wisdom it can lead to a philosophical journey. The difference between an illiterate and literate is that an illiterate can retain common sense while a literate loses even that in the name of education. Until unless intelligence transforms into wisdom, we fall prey to our intelligence, because it induces a false sense of knowledge. A child can learn anything more easily at a tender age because of innocence and no preexisting impressions are coming in the way of learning. Learning a new language is tough for grownups while kids can catchup more easily. Even to embark on a spiritual journey, our pre-existing impressions are stumbling blocks. We need to unlearn a lot to conceive the truth, overcoming our colored vision. Our mind is least troubled in innocence and wisdom, while it troubled most in between in the name of intelligence. I came across many giants like scientists, doctors and IIT graduated engineers and alike with their high intelligence embarking on a spiritual path upon culmination of their intelligence into wisdom that humbles us. False sense of knowledge is a liability from intelligence, while wisdom is truly realizing our ignorance. This world is largely meant for those with mediocre intelligence.

What we know is infinitesimal while what is not known to us is infinity.

Self-esteem

This is an expression of self-respect striking a balance between self-pity and ego. One who believes in self-respect neither stoops down for his gains nor insults others for his wants.

Mechanics of Mind

Mechanics of Mind

In my childhood when I had grown enough my parents wanted to put me in school. The moment I came to know of this, I became jittery and started crying like mad. But my parents didn't give in, despite the firm resistance I had shown. I was dragged along and was dumped in school. The whole day I spent weeping silently. Realizing that I would be sent to school without my consent, out of inevitability I became quiet and was attending, swallowing my bitterness. As the days passed by my peer group befriended me and I started mingling with them slowly. We spent playing around in leisure hours and I got used to their company so much that I started cursing myself staying at home even on weekends. We feel homely, comfortable in an environment we are used to and this comfort zone of mind is conditioned for a given environment which makes us resist our exposure to anything strange to us which by and large influences our life, by influencing our line of thinking in making our choices. Right from the dishes, we choose when we visit a restaurant to the level of career we choose is influenced by this conditioned thinking.

We boasted of landing on the moon, our trials to land on Mars, exploration of galaxies, and in search of extra-terrestrial life too. But we do not mind our mind and are carried away with it, and we don't feel the force of thought. It's like when you travel in a train, the pace of the train isn't felt because you are being carried along and you feel stationary. As we are also carried away by thoughts we don't feel the force of it. Thoughts are repetitive so also the actions, which is due to the conditioning of the mind. Conditioning of the mind represents the mechanical nature of the mind. It is the result of past perceptions and beliefs as well that bring about the same reaction in a given situation. Though it is devoid of discretion it is based on the principle of known evil is better than unknown angel which is presumed as a survival mechanism and our longing for sticking to familiar things to feel secure despite proof otherwise.

In physical terms, I prefer to describe the mind as a blend of matter component and energy component. The matter is rigid while energy permits expansion and or transformation. When the body is described as a physical matter, I would rather describe the mind as a matter and energy transitional zone. The energy component of the mind shows free will while the matter component is rigid with a conditioned mind as a result. More repetitive the action more conditioned it becomes and vice versa.

When we become observant of thoughts (which is possible when you don't get carried away by them) instantly you feel the force of thoughts, the more you observe, the frequency and intensity of thoughts start declining, consequently as you remain as spectator thoughts do not result in action. This is how deconditioning of mind emerges merely 'by observation' which is nothing but meditation. This is where your 'WILL' begins.

However much we understand someone's preaching or even from past lessons we can't change the line of thinking because of rigid conditioning of the mind. If I'm permitted to say rigid mechanical matter component of mind can acquire more of plasticity and elasticity on adapting to witnessing of thoughts crossing mind. Probably this is why when things are enforced on the mind when it's rigid and not plastic or elastic enough it's aptly described as mental 'break own' because it is solid and inert that breaks. *Rigid or matter component of mind focuses on sustenance while elastic or energy components await adoptive means and paving way for evolving in our plane of thinking.*

It is need of the hour to allow the elastic component to expose to stranger mental environment by admitting exposure to stranger thoughts and experiences in a state that is devoid of preconceived notions. It is impossible to negate impressions imprinted but the other way around is simply to watch them occurring without fuelling them with action or by perpetual thinking. More watchful you become more feeble thoughts become and with consistent practice they may even cease to occur. Now the mind is like a clean slate on which you can rewrite as you wish. While past impressions brought about conditioning, now current perceptions leave behind edited version that prevents conditioned behavior and admit willed behavior.

In simple terms meditation is deconditioning of the mind that is refreshed and formatted for further configuration. Physical evolution has progressed enough from unicellular organisms to the level of ape-man or even man.

Now it's the turn for mental evolution. We would've met all our biological needs without ever needing a thinking faculty like animals with their instincts. To exist and coexist in the highest order is what evolution is destined to be. This self-destructive so-called scientific advancement or urbanization can't mean evolution. Urbanization can't be equivalent to socialization or civilization. Instincts are conditional for mere survival that helped animals for eons. We can't remain in the same zone.

Matter components go on diminishing in proportions as the elasticity of the mind emerges from deconditioning by meditation. The body belongs to a 3Dimensional material world. Like the 4th dimension that makes its appearance in time, we exist on different planes when we transcend this physical consciousness. The mind is analogous with time. More we watch thoughts more we become unattached, less we belong to past, more we belong to present...a time travel rather...we may peep in the future too, but meditation teaches the art of enjoying 'being' and saves us from the agony of 'becoming' which is the cause of stress all through the life.

There are no physical tools to deal with the mind. Mind alone can help to transcend the mind...provided, you are not carried by the river of thoughts but by sitting on the bank of this river watching it passing by. Like wind resistance by itself resists flying of bird but the same resistance helps fly higher when it flutters wings against the wind, the mind itself offers resistance to go beyond and mind alone can facilitate going beyond the mind

Sensory perceptions yield instincts by repeated exposure that are meant for meeting biological needs including survival. We can't confine to these instincts as we have thinking faculty. But this thinking, where is it leading us to. we proclaim that humans are the most intelligent of all species. Then what is this intelligence for? can we equate it with scientific advancement? Giant of science Albert Einstein himself committed saying "I fear the day that technology will surpass our human interaction. The world will have a generation of idiots".

Instincts spring from matter component or inert component of mind that serves for survival. Intelligence springs from a negotiable elastic component of the mind that's meant for adaptation which is an inherent part of evolution. But at the plane of humans what is expected out of evolution? when a species can exist in the highest order of manifestation that can survive longer,(without the aid of so-called advanced medical sciences)happier (as we are endowed with a mind that is unprecedented in the rest of species)with natural endowments at a plane higher than animals, we can probably call it evolution. Intelligence is means, not the end. Where intelligence culminates, wisdom emerges.

Transcending physical consciousness is transcending matter that is 3 dimensional and transcending the mind is transcending the 4th dimension as the mind coexists with time and analogous with it., which is a transition zone between absolute and relative worlds. Reaching the absolute while physically existing could probably mean evolution. Absolute here means beyond relativities like good and bad, higher and lower, joy and sorrow or any such attributes.

We need to evolve further with natural endowments without any aid of tools designed by science, be it for biological needs, health, or happiness. Living healthy has to be a natural course of life and living longer or a natural span of life of species also must be a natural endowment. But we differ from the rest of the species by living happier which is a manifestation of the mind. After all, all the thinking processes and all endeavours in life are in search of happiness end of the day. The insecure feeling is an intense desire for security in exaggerated proportions. This can be overcome by a shift of mental plane from rigid (conditioned) zone to elastic (deconditioned) zone that helps in adapting to newer domains and dimensions of life. Stress in simple terms is the inability to adapt to a given situation. Anxiety, depression, neurosis spring from the inability to cope with the given situation. These are dealt with medication that alters neurochemistry of the brain, in other words, they deal with the effects of anxiety depression, or neurosis but not with the cause.

Here lies the crux as meditation deals with the cause, which is the inability to adapt. Adaptation in other terms is nothing but being happy under given conditions. This paradigm shift is possible only by way of meditation that facilitates unveiling of conditioned mind layer by layer leading to a 'virgin' state of mind that is open for welcoming changes leading to a better moulding. A mere understanding of the literal meaning of words like 'think positive' or 'be positive' can't bring about a change for adaptation in the mental plane. It is high time we explore the mind not by physical tools but by being conscious about the mind to have deep insight like we can have a better sight of the bottom of the lake once ripples of water on the top settle.

In the above narration, I attempted to explain the reason for the conditioned mind and comfort zone and tried to characterize the mind with the rigid and flexible component where the rigid mind is persistent about existence while the flexible component persistently asks for evolution (going and growing further).Rewiring of the brain is possible only after deconditioning which is not by physical means, but only through meditation. It is like emptying a vessel before we fill it with desired or intended contents. Fundamentally insecurity is driving us mad which is mainly because of the conditioning of the mind. The more open we become to changes encountered, the more adoptive we become. More adoptive we are, less stressful or insecure we feel. Saner we become in our thought, word and deed.

Meditation is not simply for relaxation or stress buster anymore. It is the need of the hour from the individual level to the level of the entire human species. Barring spiritual and philosophical aspects it is very much needed not for evolution alone, but we reached a point where we need it for our very existence. No species in nature has a self-destructive attitude except humans. The irony is being aware of this fact we hardly attempt to correct ourselves. Beliefs in arbitrary boundaries, greed, and selfishness, false values are still driving us mad. The chaos started in mind and it has to end in mind only. No physical measures can help us out. Consequently, meditation remains to be an absolute need and absolute choice too. It's high time that we need to view it without religious or ritualistic colours.

Bridging science and spirituality is possible in the mental plane as physical sciences and physical senses have their limitations that come in the way to comprehend anything that is beyond the physical level.

Possessiveness

Possessiveness is not a noble virtue as believed. It is a sort of insecure feeling attached to a person or a thing. The only one who is confident that what he deserves will be his always will never be possessive.

A balanced mind acts, a mind with polarities reacts

When you see people arguing, the voice of the one who has no point in his or her argument will be in high pitch. Those who think less, react more. Avoiding an argument is greater than winning an argument. The One who wins the argument is a loser. A balanced mind sees no point in the argument, or when compelled to put forth, it can only be discussion, but never an argument. Arguments are meant for argument's sake and those who argue only intend to win an argument, not to prove their point judiciously. This again is because of deep-rooted convictions, likes and dislikes, ego, and self-centered thinking. There has never been a fair intention in arguments in either of the parties.

This reminds me of an anecdote from Osho's writings. He says lovers who truly love each other when together can communicate with each other even in silence, or even when spoken in a low tone or even whisper is more than enough to convey their feelings. But when we watch a couple who are not close to heart each other, even if they scream can not convey what they feel to each other. This happens because there is some expectation or polarity or predefined standards in mind which are expected in their partner to comply with which may not be the same for another partner. Due to these polarities, there is often a ruckus between a married couple. Even high-pitchedvoices also can't communicate what they want while a couple in love can communicate even in silence because their thoughts are unified in total acceptance of what they are. When there are preconditions to accept, it creates polarities and brings in more heat than light in their relation.

Lovers till they marry, their common agenda is only to get married, hence no hassles. But once married true agenda is highly variable, and each has their own that may not concur with each other.

It is the quality of a composed mind to remain calm, while the weak mind reacts. If Pandavas were to retaliate in every humiliating condition by Kauravas they would have lost to Kauravas much before Kurukshetra. A balanced mind is achievable with due experience and exposure in life and of course, it is a reward from meditation when consistently practiced. Even in our minds conflicts creep in and debate goes on. What is once yes, another moment it is no. The mind is swept away by positive and negative thinking.

Polarities mean positive and negative and attraction and repulsion and a balanced mind is said to be in a neutral state...Attraction and repulsion towards a person or a choice in career or anything for that matter we come across or even ina given situation are because of impressions made in mind by our belief or through our past experiences. Polarities of mind I mean here are our likes and dislikes. All that we like may not be worthy enough or all that we dislike may not be unworthy. Our beliefs and opinions decide our choices while facts decide the outcome. It never means that we are always wrong in opining things but one must keep in mind that things or possibilities are sometimes beyond what we presume. Being open-minded makes you act according to situational demand rather than action originating from our pre-existing impressions which is rather a reaction most of the time. Being watchful and observant takes a lot of patience and it's a mental task not to get yielded to pre-existing impressions and to see things as they are.

Starting from individual beliefs to beliefs in society, religious beliefs, every preformed idea or belief, or even belief in science alone (not beyond) blinds us indeed to the truth. Precious opportunities in life to realize the truth or to seek truth to see the things as they are, be it a person or place or career or whatever is overshadowed in the darkness of our beliefs.

Another most taxing thing because of these impressions is, all our thoughts originate from these pre-existing impressions and our relentless thinking that goes on and on endlessly is fueled by these impressions. More the impressions in mind more the troubling thoughts and vice versa. On these grounds I say meditation helps in erasing these impressions layer by layer, consequently, our reactions also are retarded gradually in frequency and intensity.

If we pay attention carefully to every thought crossing the mind, it's almost always concerning our memories, ambitions, fears, inhibitions, regrets, and so on. Until these scars heal thoughts almost always revolve around them and these dissipating thoughts necessitate clearing these scars or impressions so that it is not so taxing to mind. The more we react in a situation due to pre-existing impressions more reinforced these impressions are. To put it another way more proactive we are less intense these impressions become and we can break the vicious cycle of impressions and actions one reinforcing the other. The cause and source of all our thinking are largely these deep-rooted impressions. In other words, this is what conditioning of the mind is. One beautiful zen quote I recall at this juncture that says '*if you are in depression you areliving in past, if you are anxious you are worried about future and if you are peaceful you are living in present'.*

All of my spiritual journey since I embarked on this path has only made me realize end of the day that living in present, rather I reframe it as living the present is the ultimate realization in life. Only an open mind lets you feel, experience, and live in present.

An open mind opens up unknown possibilities and a conditioned mind curtails possibilities.

Even in our day-to-day interactions, we are eager only to express ourselves and give a deaf ear to what others say.When someone is talking to us, we are more eager to react in our own way saying what occurs to our mind rather than listening to them. We are more interested in giving suggestions to others than listening to anyone, however wise another person may be. Listening needs an open mind. Listening not only is a gesture showing respect to one who is talking to you, but it also enriches our knowledge. When we talk we only talk of something that we already know, but when we listen it's quite possible to get to know many things that we never knew before. Observing, listening with an open mind, without the interference of our pre-existing impressions, if not anything it can at least prevent us from being inappropriate in a given condition.

Let's guard ourselves against our own opinions as they are not necessarily facts always. Unfortunately, half the life is spent, carrying borrowed ideas, impressions and opinions and what is much needed is actually is unlearning what is learned with or without our consent all through.

Lust

Lust is not simply a projection of the mind. It is a biological need strongly expressed in nature for sustaining species, but oppression and social dogmas on sex lead to an ugly expression or even gratification. Animals copulate only to procreate. But in humans sensual pleasure probably intended to lure opposite sex. This sensual pleasure when matured can be conjugal bliss.

Meditation brings us closest to present

Meditation is NOT ritual

Meditation is NOT just about mental relaxation

Meditation is NOT about controlling the mind

Meditation is NOT concentrating on something

Meditation is NOT doing something

Meditation is NOT doing anything

Meditation is a passive phenomenon

Meditation is primarily unlearning process, but not learning

Like you can't fall asleep by effort, you can't meditate by an active effort.

Meditation is a way of self-realization, realizing what we are and what we are not.

It is like allowing ripples of water in a lake to allow mud to settle for crystal clear sight of the bottom of the lake.

For those who find meditation difficult, I suggest two simple mental exercises that can be tried and see if they work. Put a smiling face (even if it is a plastic smile) as often as you can remember. With a smile on your face, you might notice your mood changing instantly making you feel better. I experienced it myself. Probably smile on a face sends a signal to the brain to bring in a corresponding mood. Just like mood brings about bodily changes, bodily movements may also bring about mood changes prospectively. I have a conviction that yoga mudras and as anas are based on this principle to bring about such mental makeup to facilitate spiritual practice.Conscious effort we need to make this smile our second nature so that it keeps us in good humor.

Another mental exercise that I suggest is, be aware and conscious of complaining mind that relentlessly keeps complaining about something or other. Be conscious about your thought, word, and deed. Stop complaining even in your thoughts about anything or anybody. Don't entertain complaints even concerning you, blaming your misfortune or bad times or anything of that sort. Complaining mind drags to keep complaining further just about anything literally starting from breakfast to lawbreakers. Practice even for a few minutes a day as frequently as possible being aware and conscious that no complaint is entertained in thoughts even about yourself. This lets you watch your thoughts and keeps a check to some extent at least to the influence of the subconscious mind that keeps us driving all day in our thinking and doing anything for that matter.

Everything that we see around is the translation of our thought

Other than nature, all that we see around is the translation of our thoughts and ideas, maybe constructive or destructive, knowingly or unknowingly they are all projections of the mind, the way it works. The malady started in mind has to end in mind only. This is when meditation comes in handy. We may be at receiving end or maybe contributory at times to good and bad happening around. A sort of insecurity driving us mad from the individual level to a global level. The Source of the problem lies in the mind. However much we take measures at the physical level, permanent solutions for many problems from the individual level to community level can't be arrived at. I heard of a quote that aptly states, life is 10% what is happening to us and 90% of how we react to it. All the content in this book is intended to highlight 'how we deal with what is happening to us'. There is no point in going on blaming people around for every difficulty or discomfort we are confronted with. Complaining becomes our second nature such that much of our thinking is about complaining about something or other that goes on and on impulsively and we almost always ignore our responsibility towards keeping ourselves happy and not to cost happiness of others by our claims. Every problem we are confronted with at personal, social and global level has its beginning in mind and will have to end in mind only (by self realization or self actualization that's conferred in meditation) Solutions proposed at physical level might serve for a brief period proving futile sooner or later.

Complaining is habitual, not always situational

Let us try a simple mental exercise to see how conditioned we are to dwell in complaints all the while.

Watch the thoughts crossing the mind briefly for about 15-20 minutes, without responding to those thoughts. Simply watch and pen down all the thoughts crossing the mind randomly now and then in a day for about 15-20 minutes. We come to know how much we are used to keep thinking negatively and keep complaining about all that we see, hear, or think like regret and complaints about past, complaints about colleagues, boss, spouse and children, job, politicians, traffic on the road, pollution, weather changes what not…hardly there is anything that you do not complain about…then how do you expect yourself to be happy, blaming your life, saying that you are not happy at all. I would say it's a psychological disorder (not in conventional terms though) to keep eyes fixed on negative aspects. One who sees obstacles focuses only on obstacles, one who sees the target, gazes his vision only on the target, and overlooks obstacles.

Complaining not only makes life lusterless but even extinguishes enthusiasm in doing what we are supposed to do., then dissipates all energy in thinking as these negative and complaining thoughts can often lead to emotions. Being at peace and open-minded improves our efficiency in our work, all the mental and physical energies are put in the right channel making the outcome more effective in our deeds. The cause of concern with this complaining nature is, it becomes almost our second nature and approach and attitude towards many things we come across and people we meet in the given context will be undesirable most of the time and it takes its toll naturally.

Love

Love is the purest of all fine feelings. Lust is that of mind while love is that of the heart (not physical). Until lust matures into love, lust keeps bothering for physical or sexual gratification.

Mental conflicts make epicenter of stress

Generally, what we think we don't speak and what we speak we don't execute. This may have various reasons. We do not practice what we preach to others or we may feel it's impractical to do something that you think of or inhibitions, hypocrisy...it could be anything. Whatever the reason is when there is a disparity in what you think, speak or do, it constantly builds mental conflicts and keeps fueling thoughts that could trouble us. If you watch carefully when you are completely engrossed in doing something that you have been thinking of, when thought, word, and deed are in the same line...you can notice your mind being in an absolutely thoughtless state. This experience sometimes is possible in listening to favorite music or if competent enough to play some instrument when playing such favorite musical instrument, while talking to loved one, sometimes while enjoying the beauty of serene nature around...that's when we dwell in that experience and mind practically involved in feeling rather than thinking and absolutely it will be thoughtless., and it is needless to say how relaxed we feel after such experiences. Further, it infers that thoughts are dissipating. One of the driving forces for such thoughts is thought, word and deed are not coaxial, which means they are not in the same line and such conflicts incessantly keep troubling us. This is indeed a sort of meditation even while being physically active to have thought, word, and deed in the same lines.

Suppose you are in a job that you can neither quit nor you can enjoy that can pile up a lot of stress eventually turning out as a source of stress constantly. There are many such examples in day-to-day life forcing us to do things that we don't like and not letting us do things that we are desirous of. We can not say no to many in many occasions when you want to say. We can not even say yes when we want to say it because, accepted norms in society, hypocrisy, lack of freedom to choose may not allow us all the time to say what we want to say.

There are two ways we adopt while dealing with such situations. One is to compromise and the other way is acceptance. A compromise is a negative approach and it's like going about doing things, as we are condemned with no choice other than one in hand, feeling helpless. But, this attitude makes it even more painful. Acceptance is rather a positive approach…coming to terms with realities, realizing our strengths and limitations with a hope that things would get better as we work on it for better prospects. Unless we accept what we are, realizing our limitations at the moment, we never attempt to improve ourselves. Compromise is a sort of unacceptance, cursing fate and cursing ourselves making things even more agonizing. The more we accept, the fewer conflicts creep intoour mind, the more productive we become and it lays the path for green pastures ahead. Acceptance paves for adaptation, adaptation keeps you stress-free and lets you pass through against odds at ease.

Thought, word, and deed when in harmony, it is said to be 'thrikaranasuddhi'(in Sanskrit)…means there is fairness in thinking, speaking, and doing and being single-minded and you are true to yourself in letter and spirit. This can rather be described as dynamic meditation which is usually possible with a still body and mind conventionally. This is one way of getting closer to the path of meditation. Another crucial mental exercise that is narrated in the foregoing lines suggests to be watchful about the nature of thoughts crossing the mind and to make note of how often negative and or complaining thoughts about something or other cross the mind. Both above practices make the day less stressful and make us watchful about the way get along with people and how we go about doing things. This prevents us from doing things that emerge from our subconscious mind which we are unmindful of most of the time. How we do is a conscious level, while what we do always has its origin from the subconscious mind. More aware we become about our thoughts, eventually, we become more and more aware about what we do and how we do too.

Many things that we do mindlessly can be checked by the gradual practice of what has been suggested in the foregoing lines. More and more proportion of subconscious mind turns conscious with above practices, more so with consistent practice of meditation. Being watchful about complaining thoughts popping up all the while and trying to keep thought, word, and deed in one line is like a warm-up exercise before we embark on meditation. What we need to realize is thoughts can never be controlled, neither we should try to…instead we need to just be watchful about thoughts crossing the mind like watching the river flowing from the river bank and when we are unmindful of this, we are always carried along stream of thoughts and hence flooding of thoughts, literally to say so.

Mind is on a constant hunt for happiness

While bodily needs are for existence and propagation namely food and sex, the mind is on the hunt for happiness relentlessly. Seeking pleasure is one way and fighting out unpleasant things is another way. Negative traits like ego, envy, superiority, or inferiority complex, emanate from insecure feelings.

The ego tries to comfort you by making you feel that you are far above others, but in fact, it is fear of losing respect or identity. Fearing the dis-respect we try to be egoistic. It is an exaggerated expression of an identity crisis. Ego is a sort of borrowed identity by being rich or famous or by skill and talent in something. We hardly believe in identity due to our imperishable virtues.

Envy comforts the mind deceitfully making you believe that success or happiness being enjoyed by others is undeserving for them and tend to believe that their success is by fluke or stroke of luck, while the same success in your life you believe, is all by your hard work and it's befitting for you. When it's a failure in your case you tend to believe that it's bad luck and you feel you are deprived of it while you deserve it.

Superiority complex is a reflection of ego while inferiority complex is out of self-pity and unknowingly we all derive pleasure in self-pity.

All above traits prevail more often than not because we never take responsibility for our deeds or failures. Unless we are very conscious of our efforts we never take responsibility. More often we are more conscious about the result than our effort. Being conscious about responsibility constantly keeps questioning our genuine interest, genuine effort and keeps alerting us when interest or effort is deficient. This makes us uncomfortable and we conveniently ignore our responsibility in many things and resort to blaming others or conditions prevailing for our hurdles and failures. Even our failures are unacceptable for us when we do not realize our responsibility in our endeavors.

Ego

Ego is an exaggerated projection of selfishness for identity. It goes far beyond self-respect or self-esteem and even at the cost of respect for others.

We go on trying to invent happiness, but it's always a discovery within

Happiness is our true nature, that's why babies are found joyful almost always unless they are hurt by some means, or when scared. *The ability of thinking is yet to disable them from being happy.* The child is in a state of bliss indeed. As we grow, behavior by instinct seen in childhood is replaced by behavior that follows a thinking pattern. More often our anxiety is nothing more than a misuse of our imagination. Regret about the past, anxiety about the future creeping in always is a reason for sabotaging happiness in present. Our futile attempts in search of happiness to find with people in our life or in places we like or in accomplishments we dream of and so on …can't even make us realize that happiness in all such things is never long-lasting. We mistake our excitement to be happy as quoted by Bhagawan Rajneesh. Excitement is always short-lived.

Whole life is spent in trying to be happy…inventing ways and means by sensual pleasures, acquiring wealth, winning over rivals…whatnot, but none of them are so promising as we think to confer happiness…only because *"happiness is always a discovery within, but never by an invention in this world around". Until we learn to be happy with ourselves and what we are, seldom we can be happy. When we are left by others its loneliness, but when you choose to be alone that is solitude. We need to evolve to this extent to experience happiness unconditionally, till then it's a mirage when we chase others or other targets in search of happiness.*

Positive thinking is not as easy as advised nor it is difficult

Anything that we speak from our own experience is knowledge in its true sense, more so in philosophical terms. However great may be philosophy put forth by so-called even salt of the earth kind of philosophers unless it is by one's own experience one need not take it for granted. Of late for many years I heard many talking about the 'law of attraction', claiming it to be the most productive experimental outcome of quantum physics. I do concur with it too, but for the mind that is embroiled in negative thinking most of the time, rather almost always…how practical it can be to completely shift thinking to another end of the spectrum, opposite pole, that is positive thinking. This law of attraction suggests dwelling in thinking or a feeling as if you are experiencing the dream that is getting materialized. It suggests visualization and to feel and to experience as if ambitions you nurture are fulfilled or dreams are materialized. This is an absolutely commendable approach indeed. But for a mind that is habitually indulged in pessimistic thinking how effectively it can switch over to this feeling by dwelling in the visualization of dreams being materialized?

Even when we attempt and try to put it into consistent practice, sooner or later mind will bounce back to our habitual pessimistic thinking. Ofcourse, this is exclusively my experience I'm talking about. Here I intend to share my experience while going about dealing with negative thinking or when in pursuit of your goals or dreams.

The moment I start working on my ambitions, my mind pops up with some queries like…am I really capable enough? Even if so, it reminds me of possible hurdles that might crop up on my way. Ranging from questioning the feasibility, possibility, and ability, it might even go to the extent of impeding my progress or even attempts with fear of failure. When we start working on something we always start with hope and enthusiasm more often, (which means we start with positive thinking, otherwise we can't even make a beginning). These negative thoughts that pop up as we go may even antagonize whatever positive thinking that we had, to start with. Polarities are polarities. Here I mean positive and negative thinking. The beauty of these ugly negative thoughts indeed is…these negative thoughts are nothing but a sort of 'checklist' reminding us to assess your capability, feasibility, and possibilities of our endeavors and reminding us to attend to those shortfalls if any while on the journey to fulfilling our dreams. But this reminder or checklist appearing as negative thinking becomes so overwhelming that we may even end up giving up altogether at times. Positive thinking or positive suggestions or visualization as suggested in the law of attraction could only last for a brief time and I couldn't practice to the extent of making it my second nature. This eventuality made me adopt a different approach that I'm going to share in the following few lines.

When I contemplate on working on something I'm desirous of, as usual, I kick start with a positive approach, and when I tried to visualize as if I have accomplished or feel as if it materialized…this state of mind was short-lived and was bouncing back to negative thinking. Many of us, almost all of us are habituated to think negatively right from the moment we wakeup in the morning as I narrated earlier. We hardly ever have the mental makeup to start our day pleasantly. Due to this conditioned negative approach that arises, triggered by our daily routine insight, perpetually, we are into negative thinking even when we meet strangers or take up new projects. Our conscious effort to think positively pulls back our mind like elastic is drawn back when left after being stretched. This is what conditioning is. Honestly, I'm unaware of how effective this law of attraction can materialize our dreams…I say I'm unaware, I do not say it doesn't work.

Instead what I do is, I never pay attention to thoughts crossing my mind, be it positive or negative, because these polarities are like stretching elastic and it's drawn back whichever way we stretch as far as my experience goes. So, I do not pay attention to any thought concerning the outcome of what I'm working on. Neither I resist negative thinking as it crosses the mind, so much so I'm not overwhelmed by positive thinking crossing the mind. I'm just indifferent to both polarities of thinking. Negative thinking dampens while positive thinking might give a false sense of security, instead I focus all my energies on the thing at hand trying to get engrossed completely in what I do, that conserves all my energy for thinking and all the energy is channelized in doing my job, being single-minded. This way when I'm giving my best, the best possible outcome is a natural consequence and it can't be otherwise. This is in a way complying with karma yoga professed by lord Krishna that endorses "do your best, leave the rest". Much of our regret in life is about 'not doing things we wanted to, due to overthinking'. This made me adopt this approach of being indifferent to any kind of thoughts crossing my mind about its outcome. This approach I adopted in personal, professional, and even social life turned my journey from a bumpy ride to a smooth sail. If I ever failed that was only when I didn't adopt this approach effectively. Visualization in the law of attraction is different from daydreaming. Many of us indulge in daydreaming mistaking it for visualization as suggested in the law of attraction. What I state here is my experience and in no way I'm contradicting the law of attraction.

Self-pity

Self-pity is a sort of escapism to face the truth and makes us ignore our responsibility or contribution to our condition. A sort of pleasure we derive by feeling sorry for ourselves.

Living in a moment is different from living for a moment

Being indifferent to our thoughts is a simple and effective means of dealing with our minds. It doesn't budge in by logic, either amenable for control by effort or our will. Fuel to thinking is thinking itself. One thought leads to another when we respond to it and it goes on perpetually. The only way to attenuate thinking is by being indifferent to it. It doesn't fuel any thinking further. This is indeed the best approach in meditation and stretching this practice while we attend to our chores and job or while indulging in any activity, facilitates 100 percent focus on the job at hand. Less and less energy will be dissipated in thinking over a period of practice. Mind is your master if yielded to it, but best servant when we take over.

Our reaction or response to every thought arising alone can fuel it, but wanes of when we are indifferent to it. This practice endows us with the blessing of living in present, in every sense. Mind is drawn to past or future, like and dislike, hate and love, good and bad, success and failure, beautiful and ugly, attraction and repulsion…likewise polarities in mind keep us spinning the thoughts., consequently line of thinking determines the course of action and we find our self in a groove all along, venturing nothing beyond, even to think.The heavy toll we are paying for this is, *missing the present*. Life is silently consumed by thoughts before we realize it. This is what is meant by living in the moment is different from living for a moment. Mind is the sense of all senses. When it isoccupied, even other senses are shut. Ears can't listen, maybe they hear, eyes lose sight, maybe they can see. That way every moment lapses without a taste of life. We just exist, we don't live indeed. To sumup all spiritual and philosophical knowledge and experience, 'being in present' is what we need to adapt. *The whole life in its entirety is available to us in the present alone. There is nothing like tomorrow. Because every tomorrow has to be today (present moment) for you to do anything you want to do.* Yesterday is getting buried in the past each day. Past is time that slipped away. Future is time that's yet to come and present alone carries all the potential of life for us to experience anything. Past is memory, future is imaginary while present alone is experience. That's why it is quoted that living in a moment is different from living (existing) for a moment, on these lines.

Gratitude

Gratitude is among the noblest virtues one can have and reverence for what we possess or are blessed with. In a way, to be grateful is to be happy.

How we do is joy, not what we do

Doing anything just for the joy of doing alone unveils the beauty of life, unleashes life in full flow. It all boils down to whatever we do, how we do matters more than what we do. There is no exception to this. The food we eat to cherish, the job we do to flourish, a relation we love to nourish...all depend on how well we are engrossed in doing them with no motive or expectations. The philosophy of karma yoga in essence is this...doing just for the joy of it. It's like discovering the joy of life *within. We go on trying to invent happiness in all that we do, but it is always a* discovery within. For the same reason meditation that involves no physical or mental activity unveils such bliss, implying that a fountain of joy is within.

We might have seen laborers working happily, talking to each other, or being playful at their work while executing their job and executives in their air-conditioned chambers with a frown on their forehead, more often. Many of us while playing games, so long we play for the joy of it, it doesn't matter whether we win or lose the game, but when we are serious about winning the game, it is no more a joy to play. The joy of riding a bicycle without support for the first time in childhood is far more a joyous experience than driving your first car for the first time in your life. Such experiences are many in life implying that how we do is a joy not what we do indeed. All our experiences in childhood stand as best examples to realize 'how we do is joy, not what you do'. The street food I had with my besties gave me more pleasure than the food I had in official gatherings in so-called star hotels. Unless we have a liking for what we do, we can never be happy whatever we do. Trivial things can make us happy when we do it with love and even so-called acclaimed good experiences can not make you happy when you are not inclined to it. What I mean here is your attitude is responsible for happiness in the end.

Ingratitude

Ingratitude is almost ubiquitous in our lives and this world. Opportunistic people tend to show ingratitude and generally feel their needs are their only priority. In a way projection of selfishness, but it's a liability all through, that can never confer lasting happiness.

We are best lawyers for our mistakes and best judges for others mistakes

The mistakes we commit do not bother us much and we have conviction most of the time that the reasons were valid enough for committing our mistakes. Similar mistakes or even trivial mistakes when committed by others, we make a mountain out of a molehill. The irony is we don't even remember committing similar mistakes while criticizing others.

A mother-in-law watching a tele serial sympathizes daughter in law being harassed in tele serial by her mother-in-law.But is unmindful of her attitude towards her own daughter-in-law in real life. A parent who curses the education system for burdening children with unhandleable stress pesters his children to study even harder. This hypocrisy not only makes us lose our integrity, blinds us to the truth. The communication gap grows wider with such double standards. When I teach my students in medical school, being a professor, I recall my days when I was a student, how I have been and try to understand their perspective while teaching so that I can connect to them better. To blame others is effortless but it's fruitless. Attempting to understand takes 'getting into their shoes' before we speak up or opine anything. Thinking that you are always right and others are always wrong makes you a loner in the end.

Belief

Belief is always a borrowed opinion or idea. We believe just because we choose to believe irrespective of facts or truth. Believing a person, or an idea, or religion is all just the matter of our choice we made to believe in.

.

An open mind opens unknown possibilities

Ignorance pays off better than intelligence at times. Intelligent thinks of too many possibilities or consequences stalling the job to be done, while ignorant is unmindful of consequences and innocently carries out the job at hand more often. I prefer not to have any presumption or assumption on the outcome of our deeds, like negative or even positive thinking. Attitude either way can influence our input and output. I believe in just doing what is in my hand and doing my part and giving my best. *It doesn't mean not planning, it only means giving the best in execution.* This approach helped medeal with many conflicting conditions in testing times where I avoided judging the complexity of the issue or even my ability to deal with it. One step ahead with an open mind unfolded next step leading to a path of success. But ofcourse, none can advocate one's own experience as the universal standard for all. *Every difficulty in our life is teaching us to grow beyond our limitations.* More often than not children from poor families have their fire kindled for better education, qualification, and social status. Here their poverty by itself is a driving force for them to grow beyond their poverty to prosperity. Most of the time it is not opportunities that decide growth but our will with an open mind that explores possibilities that proves productive.

This open mind concept reminds me of an incident when I was a general practitioner. This anecdote might feel like an offbeat example, but still, I wish to share. One young boy who recently got married consulted me complaining of erectile dysfunction that was agonizing him, that too during the recent days of his marriage. Too much speculation about sex life, misinformation, impractical expectations take their toll in this domain in the lives of many. He was prescribed some aphrodisiacs by indigenous practitioners and was even counseled by psychologists trying to make him realize that it was psychogenic., but all this turned out futile. Fear and anxiety blunt discretion, which is why even when he was counseled to realize it was psychogenic, it couldn't prove effective. I simply suggested him not have any agenda in his mind while going for making love with his wife. I suggested even not to have positive thinking that would probably mount the expectations and naturally advised not to have even negative thinking. Suggested him just to spend with his wife in bed without an agenda and to get into some involving conversation while caressing now and then and advised him to practice this for a few days. A few days later without him being conscious about it, they got intimate physically and he could overcome his performance anxiety. When the mind is not obsessed with the result, the best results are likely.

Stress felt by students is not because of studies, but to large extent, it's because of their worry about examinations and their outcome. If the focus is on studies neither there will be any time nor need to worry.

Simple advice or suggestions like…'don't think negatively' as advised by many or even by psychologists while counseling, simply doesn't serve any purpose, the reason being we can't resist a thought. Even if we try to resist, it rebounds. The ideal approach is not to resist negative thinking, but by being indifferent to it.

An anecdote from Mahabharata depicts this single-mindedness, focusing on the jobat hand and nothing else. Dronacharya while teaching archery to his pupil among

Kauravas and Pandavas, he questions each of them while targeting arrows what do they see while aiming the eye of the bird perching on top of a tree. Each of them says they see branches leaves, then a bird, and then eye, while Arjuna says he sees nothing but the eye of the bird alone. Undivided attention and such single-mindedness let him hit the target straight as nothing else is in his sight. A winner sees the target alone and nothing else, while a loser sees obstacles between him and the target

A meditative mind is also like a pulled arrow that is aimed at super consciousness, unfettered by the mundane world. A meditative mind doesn't let you get disturbed by day-to-day affairs in the mundane world and sees things beyond to find happiness. It prepares the mind such that you see no reason to worry. Our general tendency is to look for reasons for not being happy always. Meditation helps us overcome this limitation. Truly the disability lies in a bad attitude. Even physical disability is not a disability as opposed to a bad attitude. How meditation facilitates many mental faculties which is otherwise not possible is dealt with further in forthcoming chapters in a lucid manner.

Faith

Faith here I do not refer to religious faith. Faith is such a perception of mind which is unquestionable, as the faith of children in parents, a student's faith in his teacher, faithful partner. The spiritual journey is all about faith in eternal truth.

Mind is a reflection of one's own experiences, while experience, in turn, is a reflection of mind

We are what we think and what we see is our perspective. We are what we seek and we seek what we are. Like begets like…same way our actions and thoughts reinforce each other. We confine ourselves to the comfort zone and live our lives in a shell, is all because our thoughts and actions form a sort of vicious cycle one promoting another one after the other. This makes life very mechanical and the scope of life is much narrowed. The question of exploration never arises at all. Exploration need not mean exploring the world or discovering an island that's not inhabited yet. Simple things also we don't even give a thought. This limitation we are unmindful of completely. The colored vision we have is imposed on us because of cultural, regional, or religious differences and also so-called financial and educational discrepancies in society. To see things as they are without a temptation to opine or to rush to conclusions is the highest form of wisdom, which is never taught in schools. One who can realize that all these differences are arbitrary and man-made then alone sanity prevails upon for right perception of things.

Overcoming the influence of such superfluous differences is possible only for the demystified mind, which is possible either by lateral thinking or open-mindedness conferred by meditation. Sight for the eyes may be the same but vision by the mind is ever expanding in the light of meditation. This vicious cycle of preexisting impressions influencing our judgment and judgments further reinforcing our impressions can be broken at the level of mind. Meditation doesn't teach anything new in life, but it helps to unlearn what is learned with or without our consent. It removes impressions layer by layer until the self is manifest that's pristine pure, with crystal clear vision.

Conditioning, prejudice, confining to comfort zone all these eventualities are because of the fact that the *mind is a reflection of one's own experiences, and experiences, in turn, are reflections of one's own mind.* You are what you think is an age-old saying, which also means or implies that transformation is possible anytime. No one changes when we advise them to change, be it their line of thinking, attitude, habits, and so on. But they only change when there is no option left, but to change. This happens only when a blow is received in the wrong direction that sets things in the right direction. Almost much of our problems are because of our carelessness, taken-for-granted attitude, and believing that we are always right in all that we do or decide. Probably to set us right we receive such blows and they are a blessing in disguise which indeed helps us to grow beyond our limitations.

One beautiful quote I came across sometime back is 'change the way you see, you will see the sea of change'. This is what exactly I meant in the foregoing lines. Meditation expands the horizon of thinking and our perceptions also will be wider and deeper. Instead of looking at things from our own perspective, we tend to perceive things as they are. Meditation facilitates a bird's eye view of any situation that leads to an understanding of all the facts leading to a situation. When the cause is understood in a wider perspective, the outcome appears more clearly in our vicinity.

Another malady of mind is procrastination. A lazy fellow always has an excuse for not doing, but achievers always look at the reason they should work for. *Procrastination or postponement in fact is, comforting your mind for not doing the job right now, but it's never a decision to do it later.*

We do not know what we do not know

Actually, the sign of wisdom is to realize more and more that we know nothing. Realizing our ignorance and limitation of our knowledge is true wisdom

As mentioned earlier, all our thoughts are aligned in lines of food, sex, and shelter. However rich we are our earnings are fundamentally for our procuring food, and all passions and inherent instinct to attract the opposite sex is for the gratification of sexual desires which indeed is meant for the procreation of species. Sexual sensual pleasure is the additional drive to desire which is eventually again is for procreation (contraception to avoid conception is irrelevant to the theme of discussion here). Striving to amass wealth and luxuries in simple terms again is the drive for shelter in exaggerated proportions.

Practically in no way do we differ from animals in our motives and instincts in spite of modern life, sophisticated culture, education, or whatsoever. I do not demean, but I say we are still primitive. Even considering the blueprint of life, the DNA, less than 3% of it alone is expressed in humans. We are boasting so much about advances in genetics, but we are still not aware of what 97% of our DNA is meant for. Considering this fact, can we even say we have advanced well in modern medicine or scaled new heights in scientific advancement? I would definitely say 'no' to this question.

Freedom is the ultimate joy we are all striving for. The desire for freedom from poverty drives us mad to make money beyond our needs. The desire for freedom from the pain of death drives you to leave behind your progeny. *But what we are missing fundamentally is what we are working on in varied proportions is merely for physical or biological needs which fundamentally no way differs from animals.* We need to realize the nature of freedom we are seeking or longing for. Freedom from bondage…bondage from wants, which actually starts for the needs. More the things we can do away with… in life, more the freedom we will be endowed with. This is the secret of joy in simplicity. Less we feel insecure, less will be things we long for when we can do away with things that we have bonded for hither to, which is synonymous with more joy of freedom in life. The joy of freedom we are in search of. This joy has nothing to do with the abundance of wealth or pleasures. Innate and our inherent quality of mind bubbles up from the bottom of mind that is ever joyful unless we disturb with our preconditions. This concept of simplicity conferring happiness is termed as minimalism, of late I heard.

I define simplicity in my own words as '*simplicity is simply realizing unwanted*'. The search for the joy of life should turn inward. We have explored enough, for this joy in all that we encountered or ran after. Mind itself should infer, we are not merely living beings like any other animal. Probably biological evolution reached its pinnacle and mental evolution is yet to be unfolded I believe.

The staggering unexpressed proportion of DNA in humans, the thinking faculty we are endowed with, prompt me to assume that it is just the beginning of the human phase in the evolution of living beings. The current intelligence of mankind is more of heat than light. Ofcourse, there is no light without heat…but to have more light than heat long way to go maybe…not sure how long or how soon. Certainly, this is not what we are or what we can be, or what we are destined to be. What is more enigmatic is no species of any animal has a self-destructive attitude. This fact is more annoying than any other and kindles a thought of introspection at large. This in fact designates the human species worse than any other species. At times I wonder or even pity humankind thinking that they are burdened with something that they are not able to handle (maddening thoughts I mean)

Scientific advances, modern life, urbanization might have just added comforts to life but couldn't actually reflect the purpose of our intelligence or thinking faculty. It couldn't bring about any elevation in the level of thinking or plane of thinking or sensibility in our thinking. Wisdom, discretionary thinking was out of focus in all the years lapsed in the name of civilization, modernization, or urbanization. Hundreds and thousands of generations have paid toll heavily to this non-discretionary mind and still paying. This may go on until our mind blossoms enough to emit the fragrance of humanity, sanity, unity in diversity, and oneness for harmonious coexistence. The will of the creator, to say so, has been the causation for this universe to come into existence and its attendant living beings. It is the manifestation of his will I suppose' from nothing to everything.Those with little inward thinking may perceive indivisibility, unity, and divinity. But there is no defined exact purpose of life as far as my perception goes.

Science always looks into utility value., and this perception may not be so gratifying for science. The direction of search by science is always outward going beyond the galaxy. Inward search is also as intriguing as outward and as boundless as outward. The outward search may have physical limitations while inward search has no limitations. It is just our willingness and inclination that can set us on the path of the journey that is boundless and endless. The more you explore more you will have to explore. Science is more thirsty for knowledge in its outward journey while inward journey involves more of realizing ignorance. More we try to know more we get to know that we know nothing. Science triggers more questions, seeking more answers, while inward journey doesn't answer all questions but rather goes on eliminating questions until you reach a point where you need no answers because there is no question left or arising. This endless 'how and why' come to a null point. This is probably because…it is not explainable but I present a few analogous ideas below

Silence is deeper than any phonation (no phonation is possible without pre-existing silence)

White color is inherently a mixture of seven colors of the rainbow (white appears colorless but it's a mixture of multi-colors)

The pivot of a rotating disc appears motionless, but that's the one to keep the disc rotating (that which appears motionless anchoring the motion indeed)

Blank paper isn't blank, but anchoring the letters inscribed on it (unless there is blank, no letter is inscribable)

Thoughtless mind is infinite rather than any ideology conceived hitherto (thoughts are like branches and leaves of the tree that spring from the imperceivable mind, like invisible root)

Invaluable things are costlier than costliest (the price of a gift presented to a loved one may be known, but the price of love is invaluable)

Everything in the universe has emerged from nothingness(the visible universeis constituted by only 5% and the rest, invisible energy, dark matter not governed by any physical laws and even beyond....in the sense what appears to be nothing has given birth to everything)

I mean to say that what appears to be nothing is everything indeed. For the same reason, almighty is beyond our perception and comprehension. Unless we elevate the plane of perception god can never be realized. What I attempted to explain in the foregoing lines is, invisible, imperceptible, and inconceivable things give rise to perceptible and conceivable things. Perceptible and conceivable things are comprehensible in the physical world, but their roots, origin are conceivable not in this physical world but a vision inward, a journey, I call meditation. On these lines a search inward alone, though not it answers every question, can let us grow beyond these questions. Growing beyond a question averts the need for an answer as the question vanishes by itself.

Trust

Belief, trust, faith all seem to mean more or less the same. But belief can be dogmatic, trust is something about the trustworthiness of a person or an idea or a concept. Trust is based on some prior experience to realize trustworthiness. Faith is beyond belief, trust, and something that never asks for proof even because it is beyond all this. Faith in truth is the best example

You are what you seek and you seek what you are

As you think so you see, as you sow so you reap, you seek what you are………all mean the same. There is an adage that says… "tell me who your friends are, I tell you who you are". The choices we make in our life reflect our level of thinking and such choices in return determine similar standards of our thinking. Elevating our level of thinking averting the influence of inbuilt impressions and the environment we live in, needs a conscious effort. More often we never feel the need because we believe that what we believe is true. Lower the level of thinking lower is the quality of pleasure we seek. A mind with a low plane of thinking goes for sensual pleasures mostly like alcohol, drug addictions, mechanical sex and allied. Those with fine feelings seek pleasure in poetry, art, music, or even relaxing in the lap of nature. When the plane of thinking is elevated choice of pleasures we seek also will beshifted from coarse to fine sort of pleasures. Sensual pleasures are short-lived. A man with the low plane of thinking preferentially enjoys only a physical pleasure with a woman and even forgets the pleasure he had and even ignores feelings of a partner once the act is done with, while an intellectual finds pleasure even in striking a sensible conversation with woman and kind of sex he can have also will be sensuous and moments are cherishable even later. No wonder a man with such a high plane of thinking may even be engrossed in platonic love that enlivens his life even when they (partners) are not together. More sensible and sensitive you become more you enjoy even trivial things in life. The smile of a child, the chirping of a bird, a cool breeze, or even a cool chat with a beloved friend sipping tea is immensely pleasurable.

We are made to believe right from childhood that to be happy, we need to achieve monumental success, monetary gains, and have all the pleasures insight. This in fact keeps us " waiting to be happy" till the end. The worst part of it is even after accomplishing all that we dream of, they prove futile in keeping us happy. These sensual pleasures and so-called success can only bring brief excitement which is mistaken for happiness which is again short-lived. Reducing the threshold for happiness such that even trivial things can make us happy is the only way for lasting happiness. In fact,the abundance of life comes from the sum of the joy of small pleasures as narrated above.

Going further, this is achievable by consistent practice of meditation. It goes on influencing such that we shed bad habits like smoking and alcohol consumption in course of time. We need not stop smoking and alcohol consumption to take up meditation, but indeed meditation by itself makes you shed these habits which are much sought after as a source of pleasure often by many. While in meditation stillness of mind (of course accompanied by stillness of body with no activity) takes us to a state of ecstasy and bliss proving that 'being happy' is our true nature, without the trouble of seeking pleasure and happiness elsewhere. A child with all his innocence is joyful, blissful, and playful without so-called stimulating sensual pleasures which makes it evident again that we are born happy. The paradox of life is though we are born happy, we go on struggling to invent happiness in something or other which by itself is a stumbling block in the path of happiness. Happiness is a discovery within always but it's never by the invention. It is not acquiring more that can keep us happy, but it is relinquishing more that paves the way for freedom and joy in life. This transformation is possible again by way of meditation, which is a boon and blessing for humankind, but grossly ignored. But it is gaining popularity worldwide, and we are desensitized to it because it originated from our motherland.

Ego, past impressions, and many such factors intrude into our perception. This can affect us by dissipating our energies in our reaction and depriving us of an opportunity for us to learn from things we are confronted with.Only aging later in life makes us realize how stupid we have been all through and what all we fought for and struggled for without an idea of how worthy they are to fight for. But aging alone is not an answer for this wisdom. We are blessed to empower ourselves with this wisdom by way of meditation. The purpose of meditation may be defined differently in different contexts. But the most relevant development in meditation is …it lets us remain in a detached attachment.

Procrastination

Procrastination is merely comforting your mind for not doing the job today, but it is never a decision to do it tomorrow.

Every problem indeed is disguised form of its own solution

Just like a caterpillar becomes a butterfly, a tiny seed growing into a huge tree against all odds…every problem we are confronted with is challenging us to grow beyond our limitations. A ship is safe on the shore, but that's not the place it is meant to be. It is like 'to exist or be extinct' when we are through this turmoil. When we resist a change and refractory to adaptation needed it only makes us more vulnerable. It is all about our willingness to deal with it.

This willingness springs from an open mind. Open mind pops up when we get our past impressions cleared…which is again is possible only through meditation. I'm taking every opportunity to highlight the importance of meditation prompting the need to realize it. Genuine problems are the ones involving our needs, but the majority are concerning our wants and optional. We need to actualize and discern our needs and wants.

The majority of the issues of our concern are only because of the importance we attach to it. Even in cases where we need to fight out or win over a situation that is impending, accepting the given conditions, without reaction, meditation lets you deal with it…as if half the war is won. Our frustration and reactions while confronting these problems are mainly because we tend to not accept the situation and become reactive making the situation worse. It is no exaggeration if I say fear of failure, fear of facing a situation by itself results in undesired outcomes. We spoil the prospects of success with our own hands due to our own apprehension. This is proved at every stage of struggle in my life. Unless there is an exposure to infection, our immune system won't be triggered. Unless hunger pangs drive you, you do not bother how to earn your livelihood. Probably problems are the way, that trigger unmasking and unleashing of our abilities. Comfort zone sooner or later engulfs you without your knowledge…by the time you realize, you are half-drowned.

Thus every problem is a blessing in disguise and disguised form of its own solution. *Avoiding a problem takes you close to it indeed* when you are left no option but to deal with it. There is no free meal in this world. Even if you are rich enough not to work for your livelihood it is costing your ability to work. I see children from 'not to do so well family' being more shrewd and adaptive, compared to those from well to do families, of course, I say this in a broad sense, not generalizing as such. Parents in rich families are indeed disabling their children from learning life skills and social skills and come in the way of adaptive mechanisms of their lives. How harm they are causing they are unaware totally or even when they are aware, they are unwilling to let their children face their odds on their own.

I came across a story that narrates natural abilities and consequences when interfered. A kid regularly watches a cocoon in their garden and to his surprise, he notices a baby butterfly struggling to break open the cocoon to swing into this external world. Unwilling to see its struggle, the kid tries to help out the baby butterfly, breaking open the shell of the cocoon to let it out. Sooner it comes out, to his surprise, it is found not being able to fly and remains meek and eventually died. When the kid cries over this, running to his father narrating what he saw, his father explains that letting it break the cocoon on its own would have strengthened its wings, enriching its natural abilities to find the way on its own to this external world.

On the same lines, though the intention of a parent is good, consequences are unpalatable quite often. Better if children learn to taste a bit of bitterness right from the beginning, they can't appreciate how sweet their success is after the struggle. I was an overprotected child in my childhood. The academic achievements of my friends never impressed me somehow, but friends with social skills and 'go-getters' impressed me a lot and I was yearning for such skills and abilities right from childhood.

Too much emphasis on academic skills subdues the social skills, and a person is incomplete without social and problem-solving skills though educated. Even an illiterate is a complete person with such abilities. This is not an overstatement on social skills or an understatement on academic skills. *We are promoting literacy, not education. We are promoting technical skills, but not life skills.*

Unless we feel how hot the sun is we don't realize how it feels in a shade. Unless we work hard, we do not realize what relaxation can mean. Unless we face failures, we do not realize the importance of success. It is also equally imperative to choose our battles sametime. What is worth fighting for is as important. More often than not many of the problems bothering us are not be solved, they are better left to be dissolved with time.

Polarities of life working parallelly, simultaneously is inherent in our lives and in nature too. Gain is associated with the risk of loss, living each day also implies moving closer to death by a day, it is the darkness that makes the light appear brighter, it is water evaporated by heat that forms clouds to shower as rain and so on…list is endless. We can't ask for one without the other. We need to have that serenity to accept. That is when we deal with harsh conditions without complaining. When we win a lottery we never say 'why me?', But when we fall sick due to some serious illness immediately we react by asking 'why me?'.

Cynic

Being cynical is conditioned thinking we are used to despite, all blessings a cynic keeps complaining about anything and everything. They are generally found mistaking their ignorance for knowledge trying to judge all they come across.

The conscious mind is just the tip of an iceberg

Fuel for thought is from the subconscious mind. Our thoughts and actions apparent to us are actually led by an inapparent subconscious mind. The less aware we are about our thought, word, and deed, the more we are under influence of the subconscious mind and life goes on without our consent at any level. We are flooded away by the force of the subconscious mind that influences our thought, word, and deed relentlessly in an unceasing manner. Our decisions, judgments, opinions, choices, likes, and dislikes are lying predetermined in the subconscious mind, and life proceeds in the same direction as determined by the subconscious mind. This in a way, I believe how predestination in the name of karma works in one's life. Along the same lines, I say, as you meditate subconscious mind is brought to the conscious level and we become more conscious about what we think, talk, or do, and subsequently, we may be bailed out from this so-called predestination. Even in the spiritual domain, it is said that a yogi has no binding with past karma. So long we are driven by the subconscious mind we are unmindful of our deeds and even misdeeds.

Melting away this concrete subconscious mind by meditation gives a fresh lease of life indeed. A rebirth is conferred. The subconscious mind is concretely programmed and our lives under its influence feel like it is pre-programmed. Meditation in a way is uninstalling this pre-existing program in mind and reprograming it at our will. This has led me to realize what fate is and how it can be averted. Probably this is one of the greatest revelations I had following meditation. For those who are in despair believing in fate or predestination, I do assure hereby that, even if such thing as fate exists it can be bypassed by reprogramming of mind with meditation.

Let me come up with a simple example in my daily routine to comprehend what this subconscious mind is and how it works. A simple example to understand this is, while we start learning to drive a vehicle we are too conscious about what we do and what we need to do, and what not to do. We will be too conscious about applying break or engaging a gear or accelerating as we operate. But, once we master driving all these operations are done without even being conscious about it and done as if it is in automation. Similarly, our subconscious mind works in automation and we are least aware of what we are doing while engaged in acts that lead my subconscious mind. The conscious mind is like our state of mind in learning stages as mentioned above that is well aware and conscious of the activities being carried out. In any learning process while acquiring desired skills reaching a level of the subconscious state is welcoming. But with reference to our temperament, disposition, inclinations, decision making, and allied features of personality, it is better not to be under influence of the subconscious mind as this robs away life from your hands and influences life in a predetermined direction without validation or evaluation of our thought, word and deed. It is easier said than done. Probably the most difficult task ever in life is to get out of the influence of this subconscious mind and be watchful and aware of our thought, word, and deed. Life under its influence is like sailing with the wind with no direction or destiny.

As I said earlier to acquire some skills like driving, swimming or operating machinery or any such skills is like a shift from conscious level to subconscious level while mastering them. But when it comes to watching our temperament, inclinations, and such impulses we need to shift from subconscious level to conscious level. Here it is more of unlearning than learning. It is the unwinding of the mind and rewiring of the brain. In simple terms what I described above is meditation. Mind by itself being mindful about the mind has to keep us reminding, to mind our mind.

Meditation goes on to increase our awareness, there by minimizing the proportion of the subconscious mind. Such conscious effort is humanly impossible to be watchful about the subconscious mind. The only resort again is meditation. There is no substitute for meditation. Nothing can parallel its efficacy. I define meditation in my own terms as a 'shift of mind in gradations from subconscious state to conscious state over a period of consistent practice'.

The process of meditation itself in simple terms involves being watchful about thoughts that are crossing the mind without being carried away by them, without reacting to them. Our reaction to thought itself fuels further thought and goes on like a vicious cycle. The moment we step back from the zone of thinking and remain in a state of observation, the force of thought ceases to influence our further thought or any reaction.

This practice while in meditation, is carried on to, day today activities and makes us watchful and aware of what we think, speak or do. This is like taking the reigns of life totally into our hands, not leaving it to fate, like sailing along with wind with no direction. This gives clarity of vision about what is and what will be, makes us more poised, less reactive, more proactive, more conservative, and a sense of mastery over whatever we do. What more we can ask for in life beyond this? No more vagaries. We take possession of the subconscious mind completely with progressive meditation, so also the life ahead. We take responsibility completely for our actions as we are completely aware of our every move. Predestination we realize to be a myth. As today makes our tomorrow and as we are taking care of today, tomorrow will also be taken care of by our vigilant conscious mind that is devoid of influence by yesterday (subconscious mind).

The subconscious mind is preprogrammed, rather programmed and it predetermines our actions so much so the consequences, that we call fate. Meditation is the reprogramming of the mind that resets the mind with configuration afresh and allows action at will. Mind the thinking faculty when mishandled is a liability that is supposedly an asset to the human species. Turning this liability into an asset is possible only by means of meditation, which is next to impossible otherwise. It is like bringing a speeding vehicle to a halt, where we can change the direction of our journey at our will. A mind that doesn't meditate is like eyes that can't see or ears that can't listen. Mind is said to be the sense of all senses, which is why it is often referred to as the sixth sense. I would rather say it is the first sense without which no other sense can sense what is. It is a way of self-actualization.

Colossal waste of time in our lives not because of doing useless things, but mainly because of dwelling in thoughts that serve no purpose. Much of life is also consumed in planning to live, rather than living.

We can't realize how much energy is dissipated by thinking until we meditate. Once we learn to meditate we wonder how we have been able to deal with this devilish mind earlier without meditation. Before getting used to meditation we are least sensitive to bother how absurd or annoying or how harsh our thoughts have been. But after certain progress in meditation, we become more conscious and more sensitive to every thought. This very vigilant and watchful attitude curbs further thinking. Until we experience the bliss in meditation during a thoughtless state of mind, however short may the span of it, we never realize, how energy is conserved by meditation. Exhaustion in thinking is checked to large extent. We become increasingly sensitive to our thoughts, feelings for others, become more empathetic, more sensitive to noise, less self-centered, and develop a sort of lateral thinking so that our ability to deal with a problem is enhanced. Negative thinking is negated, become more open, more adoptive with more acceptance of our flaws if any what so ever and even flaws in others viewed empathetically making us wholesome in every way. That's why I say this is not just a stress buster. Destressing is only a byproduct, the main product being personality transformation. No amount of preaching by any philosopher or a guru can transform anybody, but it is possible only by self-actualization which is made possible by way of meditation.

There are many more health benefits in addition to personality transformation. Memory depends on concentration, concentration depends on interest, interest depends on attitude. This attitude is taken care of by meditation. Not just by attitude changes, the mind becomes more open, more clear with minimal preexisting impressions which also favors memorizing more effectively. Clutter in mind is cleared for better vision.

Besides these, stress hormone cortisol levels are decreased which minimizes the proneness for diabetes and boosts up the immune system as well. Also brings down the activity of the sympathetic nervous system, thereby reducing blood pressure, heart rate, the burden on the heart for pumping blood is reduced. Decreases oxygen demand by the cells in the body there by reducing free radical production, which is responsible to a large extent for aging. Also improves the tone of the parasympathetic nervous system, causing vasodilatation, improving circulation. The majority of the cases of erectile dysfunction are psychogenic. Instead of relying on aphrodisiacs, consistent practice of meditation can confer a lasting solution correcting erectile dysfunction.

Going further… our cells in the body divide constantly and before cell division takes place DNA replicates itself to be passed on to daughter cells. While doing so, a small portion of DNA at its terminals is not replicated, which is carried out further by an enzyme called 'telomerase'. Our aging changes are also attributable to a fall in activity of this enzyme, consequently, terminal DNA is not entirely replicated resulting in senescence (aging) which is due to a fall in the number of cells produced compared to cells being shed. Meditation is found to enhance the activity of even this telomerase, thus retarding the aging process. Even for insomnia (sleeplessness), anxiety neurosis, depression meditation shows promising results showing improvement in the neurochemistry of brain cells.

Without reference to any studies conducted or literature concerning meditation, I shared my own experiences at this juncture. The threshold for pain is increased greatly such that pain can be born at ease. Gustatory sensation (sense of taste) also increased making food more relishable. Anorexia (lack of appetite) and hyperorexia (abnormally increased appetite) are optimized. Quality of sleep improves tremendously and hours of sleep needed also will be reduced. The threshold of sensual pleasure in sex is minimized such that even gentle touch arouses libido, improves significantly the strength of penile erection, delays ejaculation, and significantly glorifies orgasm. Those who find gentle touch and caressing more pleasurable can have an exalted orgasm, which is because of their lowest threshold in sensual pleasure. Bringing down the threshold of this sensual pleasure is made possible with the due practice of meditation. Perception of every sense is glorified and makes it immensely pleasurable. (In a humorous note I keep saying to many, sex is more of a cephalic act, not phallic, which means the largely sexual act is governed by the mind and sexual organs are only end organs where it culminates) Meditation in nutshell brings about bodily changes, changes in the mental plane, changes in interpersonal relations thereby improving quality of personal, professional and social life and a harbinger of our spiritual journey. Changes observed are phenomenal. I could believe it only because I experienced myself. All these benefits are at no cost. Imagine the gift of nature and how blessed we are to have this ability to meditate. It is just the willingness to meditate with perseverance that is enough, without giving up early. Many believe at the outset that it's not their cup of tea. This disbelief is enough to deprive you of oceanic changes that we are otherwise entitled.

To put it in a simpler way I can say meditation makes us realize who we are and what we are. It's a wonderment, amusement, and bliss, the experience of meditation is. Progressing further may enlighten us more about oneness, equanimity, cosmic consciousness, and so on. Self-centered thinking, ego, envy, vengeance all such negative shades start vanishing gradually over a period of time which is truly a transformation. But the paradox is, with all these expectations if you start meditating it may not be effective. *Meditation is to be practiced just for the joy of it. All other benefits of health are natural developments alongside.* This indeed teaches us to do things just for the joy of doing it. We are not used to doing anything without a motive generally. As I mentioned in the foregoing lines, 99 out of 100 problems are because of either selfishness or ego, other than problems concerning basic needs.

Basic needs and beyond, humans crave for

Hunger for food, sexual drive, need for a comforting shelter are understandable. But why do envy, ego, selfishness, vanity, pride, vengeance, and alike traits bother us? This is more intriguing to know. Either not readily answered or what is answered is not agreeable for many.

Selfishness is a defensive mechanism of mind that drives you to take care of yourself at any cost. But when exaggerated that could even cost viability or existence of others. Completely being selfless can also cost your own existence. Here again like I said earlier we need to draw a line on how far we can be selfish. To the extent your needs are taken care of you can be selfish. But when your wants are at the cost of the needs of others, then it is condemnable. The selfishness that is asking for beyond the needs turns into greed.

Ego is some kind of drive for self-identity. Selfishness to an extent is to take care of physical needs, but ego is a mental need that asks for an identity. You feel like standing out among others to be noticeable or praiseworthy. To the extent that you do not allow others to look down upon you is welcoming. But when you want to look down upon others to prove your supremacy over others you crossing the line. It is understandable so long your concern is self-respect. But when it is at the cost of respect for others it is condemnable. So long you want to prove yourself to others and expect their approval of what you do or desire, you wouldn't be living your life.

The best quote I ever read, shattering the ego is…

Nobody is superior

Nobody is inferior

No two are equal either

You are you, I'm I

(quoted by Osho)

Vanity or pride is a false perception of mind where you try to enjoy a worshipped image of yourself by virtue of some possessions. It is a borrowed image of yourself. When you are not so confident of your self-worth, you try to gratify your mind with such borrowed esteem of your image by some possession of wealth, or so-called education, or some skill or talent where self-worth is missing.

Daydreamer

Daydreamer keeps dreaming and never believes in his dreams coming true, but simply enjoys dreaming. This is a virtue of lazy people, in general, hoping for a miracle to happen to change their lives

Contentment is not containment

A picture is worth a thousand words. In the cartoon picture you see here, one in the first place is a bit complacent, while one in the second place is flaunting the medal.

Achievements do not really make us happy all the time. It is the attitude of gratitude for what is achieved and contentment that brings joy. I do not mean one need not aim further in achievements. Being happy with what we have and always giving our best in our endeavors is what is desirable.

We can see many employees longing for promotion for years and after being promoted, cursing themselves for a load of work and its attendant responsibilities with the designation. Such things happening is a common sight in the lives of many we see around. Do not ever attach happiness to any kind of achievement. Achievements excite us for a while and thereafter we are pulled back to routine and our habitually complaining mind starts complaining about something afresh robbing the joy of life from time to time.

Many times when some clients come to me for counseling for anxiety and depression that trouble them frequently, the first suggestion that comes out of my mouth is…you are as anxious as selfish you are. This may sound strange, but when you are too concerned about yourself, being too cautious makes you anxious and lose the discretion about 'what to worry about or to what extent to worry about. Being too selfish makes us greedy and we lose sight of contentment which is the only remedy for all our greed. When we lack that contentment we can never be happy however rich we are, healthy we are…or whatever we are. Being content is not for sainthood but it's a precondition to be happy.

Greed indeed is more in those who feel more insecure. Those who labor all day for merely their daily wages, to make their livelihood are found many a time happier than corporate executives. Life doesn't perish in poverty, but with a poor attitude, it does. Coming to the definition of success in life I only say that ' it is all about, how happy you are', but never about how rich or prosperous or authoritative you are. Life asks for more amusement rather than achievement. Unfortunately, our thinking faculty, the mind instead of making life wiser and simpler, made it more complex. The unwinding of this mind is possible only again through meditation. The wisdom of a tranquil mind is greater than the intelligence of a thoughtful mind. I'm not overstating if I say meditation is an absolute need for physical, mental, social, and spiritual well-being, which is the exact definition of health given by the world health organization.

Few lines of a moral story I'm reminded of at this juncture. There was a gardener in the King's palace who use to take care of the garden with all the joy and enthusiasm. He was always found to be enjoying the job, giving his best expecting nothing in return apart from wages he was paid. King used to wonder at his attitude and expresses the same to his minister while taking a stroll in the garden. He expressed to him saying that he is not as happy as his gardener, with all his wealth and riches, being a king, and was surprised to find him so happy being so poor. He couldn't kill his curiosity and asked his minister what keeps his gardener so happy and same time what keeps him unhappy. Minister with a smiling gesture throws away 99 gold coins that are scattered across the garden and asked the king to watch what is going to happen. The next day to his surprise gardener finds a few gold coins there one after other. He goes on searching all around and finally succeeds in finding all 99 coins. Still, he isn't found happy, he thought that there must be another coin that is missing and strives hard in searching but in vain. The next day onwards he was attending to work being absent-minded always looking around, expecting one more coin to find as he assumed that there should be 100 coins. The joy and enthusiasm he had while working altogether vanished and was haunted by his thoughts about that one missing coin.

King notices all this and finally says his doubt is cleared and his questions are answered. So long gardener was content, meeting his needs he was happy. Finding 99 gold coins itself was an unforeseen fortune, but that couldn't let him be happy and kept him driving in the search for one more, paying all the price for his greed losing the joy he had in his contentment.

Vengeance or vindictive nature, envy, and greed arise from too much self-centered thinking. One cannot be completely selfless, but there is a thin line between being selfish and taking care of oneself. The best part of it is, when one is lacking self-confidence or self-esteem and feels insecure, then alone these tendencies resurface. These are all projections of mind that no other animal suffers from. Of all these virtues selfishness to an extent is understandable. Rest are in fact befooling ourselves. Our mind, the thinking faculty which is an asset to humans turns into a liability because of these virtues. Life is beautiful as such but, we make it miserable with our imposed and borrowed standards. Understanding the origin and cause of these tendencies at the root level in deep introspection can bail us out from these maladies of the mind. So long you are carried away by these ideas, it will be an endless agony. Gratitude and contentment do not hinder you from being ambitious. They only prevent from being avaricious.

Prejudice

Prejudice is an extended belief. Prejudice and belief as it sounds need not be judicious. This prejudice can be seen from an individual level to a communal level.

Meditation settles all your agitation

Every thought if we watch, springs from opinions we carry, opinions are formed following the impressions left by our experiences in life. Meditation alone takes you beyond thought and goes on erasing impressions left in past, though we can't undo the past. In simple terms, the past ceases to influence you anymore. Even for all these maladies of mind panacea is again meditation. You gradually shed all these traits and remain in a zone where you enjoy self-respect due to self-worth, being conscious about respect deserved by others. This indeed is truly a transformation. Actually, these are mystifying layers of mind and meditation demystifies all this and what remains is what you are…what actually you are. For this reason, transformation following meditation is aptly described as self-actualization. Going further, you respect the life of every living being, realizing that they too deserve the same place as us in this creation. Once you experience that oneness that is ever-expanding, it evaporates all negative shades of mind depicted in the foregoing lines. Our mental energies are so high that we are not able to channelize them properly, nevertheless, they find their way, sometimes even with a self-destructive attitude. Out of my own meditational experience, I say mental energies are best channelized by way of meditation. There is conservation of these energies, a balance between polarities of mind.

The entropy of mental energy can be minimized, (energy being wasted on unwanted thoughts can be conserved) if I can take the liberty to say so. In addition to all the above health benefits, it lets you remain in a state of bliss that is found within. It is more magical, mystical, and more addictive than narcotics I believe, while it helps shed every other addiction. This is the impact of meditation on body and mind and further possibilities are inconceivable as of now. I'm highly optimistic about the impact of meditation that can be caused from the individual level to the human species.

But while practicing meditation, when we are too conscious about its effects and results, the mind gets distracted and this by itself can be a cause for delayed or no results or results that are less effective. We need to do it just for the joy of doing it. This approach for meditation also teaches that we need to do things just for the joy of doing it and results are taken care of in their natural course. Doing anything just for the joy of doing it always gives the best possible results. So long we are result-oriented the sanctity in execution is lost that is not as productive.

I wish to share my experience of meditation, which need not be your experience too. One's progress and experiences in meditation are not comparable to others. No path or cult or spiritual community can be claimed to be superior toothers. Each has its own path. I can even say each individual may find his own path. I do not even believe in the guru and sishya (teacher and pupil) concept as far as the spiritual journey is concerned. At least my experience is, I was disappointed upon approaching many so-called claiming to be gurus. There is no learning in the spiritual path, but there's only unlearning I say, from my experience. It's purely an inward journey

Meditation is probably I can say is the noblest of the gifts given by God to humankind. One of the prime intentions of writing this book is to share my experiences of meditation for the benefit of readers. When I was desolated after my graduation due to the uncertainty of my career I was sinking into a sort of depression and conventional medication was not much of a help to me. I use to be exhausted by my troubling thoughts and when these agonizing thoughts reached their pinnacle, it so happened that one fine day suddenly I felt calming down of mind as if we relax after vigorous physical activity, Being watchful of this I simply sat in a corner of my room and was watching thoughts settling down. It lead me to a state of thoughtlessness and I felt completely rejuvenated following this episode.

I didn't know that this was actually meditation. Later of course I was motivated and got initiated into meditation by my close friend. The soundness of mind, quality of thinking, clarity, and purity of mind were very much obvious after considerable practice. It is no exaggeration if I say almost every word written in this book was made possible only because of this meditation. I hardly ever studied books concerning yoga, meditation, or any other scriptures prior to that.

I am least hesitant to say...it is a panacea for most of the sufferings in life, be it concerning personal life, professional life or social life, or many of the issues concerning health. At least in my life, there is not a single issue that I could not resolve with the help of meditation but, I emphasize again that results are proportionate to faith. The more you surrender to the universe more meditative you become. Meditation should be a process that enables you to lose yourself (losing I ness, the ego) in gradations over a period of time with consistent practice. when meditation is done just for the joy of doing the results are profound.

Yoga is being taught widely in pursuit of physical fitness and well-being, and those practicing are confining largely to yogaasanas because it can be taught by physical demonstration and for the same reason learners can pick it easily. So far so good but, many take to yoga practice and confine only to asanas and not progress further into meditation. Many believe they cannot meditate, some give up in the middle, and much focus remains only on asanas. Even yoga teachers cannot instruct learners as effectively as they do for asanas because it can not be demonstrated as such. All these limitations retard the progress in practice from yogaasanas to meditation. By and large, meditation is a mental phenomenon and a lot of communication gap is likely to intervene between teacher and learner. Unless one comprehends the concept one can't put it in practice precisely.

I prefer to call it a passive process and there is nothing like active learning when it comes to meditation. There are of course innumerable methods, gurus, cults, and beliefs. I believe that there is nothing like a prescribed way of meditation and no one can claim theirs is the only effective means. Whatever be the method to pursue meditation, the bottom line that is universally applicable to any of these methods is …one should be indifferent to thoughts cropping in mind incessantly. Another golden rule is that one should never make an attempt to control the mind. Maybe you are surprised but, it is a fact that there is nothing like controlling the mind. The more you try to control more it rebounds and is always counterproductive. Even instructors must be keen enough not to use the term 'control the mind'.

Some advocate chanting of mantra, some to focus on breathing, and some other suggestions to focus eyes on some lamp keeping eyes open. Whatever method suggested, these instructions are only not to give much room for incessant thoughts and the prime objective is not mantra or breath or any other instruction in various methods advocated.

Thoughts keep flooding, more so while in meditation. The only suggestion I have is 'do not respond to any thought or idea' crossing the mind. When you respond to one thought, a response by itself invokes another thought and leads to perpetual thinking. Be like a spectator watching your thoughts like watching a movie. While doing so you do not identify yourself in those thoughts and step back a bit from the line of thinking watch them pass. When we do not respond thoughts are not fuelled further and gradually cease in their intensity and frequency. With consistent practice over a period, one could experience a "thoughtless state of mind or thoughtlessness" ranging from few seconds to minutes depending on the level of practice.

Initially, we feel tranquillity and serenity for those few moments. Cumulatively over a period of time, we remain in this tranquil state throughout the day, not only during the session of meditation. But how long it takes to progress to this extent is highly variable from individual to individual due to differences in adaptability, a motive for meditation, commitment, and allied factors. One can not keep on assessing progress on a daily basis and such attention for results makes the practice ineffective. Another golden rule is 'to meditate for the joy of meditation'. This in a way is the first step in life towards 'doing things merely for the joy of doing' with no motives, for those taking to the spiritual path.

It is not just about stress relief, mental relaxation, and tranquillity, but meditation gradually alters mental configuration and our perception of the external world and perspectives of life are completely transformed, of course not without a reason. As we learn to be indifferent to our thoughts our impulsive behaviour in a given condition is checked gradually. We realize not to opine things instantly so that we learn to be not hasty to react in a given situation, that way preventing us from acting in a manner that we would regret later. This allows the dawning of wisdom on a new horizon.

This very practice of being indifferent to our thoughts prevents us from yielding to pre-existing ideas in our mind pertaining to our beliefs and misbeliefs and culminates in deconditioning of mind. This development facilitates easy learning of things that we wish to learn and unlearning of certain bad practices (even to de addict tobacco or alcohol consumption). Clarity and coherence in thinking are achieved over a period of practice so that ability to concentrate is enhanced. Proportionately memory power is enhanced. Analysis, judgment becomes more discretionary. We become less self-centered, worry less consequently, and empathetic towards people around us. Much of our stress is because all our thoughts are self-centered.

I don't mean to say we become completely selfless but we get rid of that overwhelmingly self-centered way of life. Infact, the *less possessive we become more we possess.*

Apart from these developments on mental planes, there will be appreciable changes in physical health, optimizing sleep, hungry, and even improving the quality of sex life, because there will be a sea of changes in metabolism, neurochemistry, and even in the nervous system including autonomous system. Apart from scientific insight with regard to health benefits meditation confers changes from the individual level to society level. Better late than never, take to meditation that makes life conservative and more productive. Going further scientist, Bruce Lipton in his book titled 'Biology of belief'has stated that what we think, be it belief or faith or conviction we have, can even bring about changes at the gene level changing the sequence of genes we are born with. Until recently or even now most of the scientists in the medical field and even doctors are of the opinion that we are victims of some genes we inherit that could probably cause some inherited diseases or disorders. It is mind-boggling even to think that changing the sequence of genes is in our hands and at our will by changing the way we think.

At this juncture, I wish to say a few words on karma. It is widely believed that karma works as universal law not sparing anyone irrespective of religious beliefs. I do concur with this to some extent.But when it comes to cleansing of karma many conveniently resort to remedial measures in the form of rituals, which are not uniformly acceptable or adaptable or may not be even affordable. An old adage says "Buddhikarmanusaram" which means our thoughts are according to our karma making it a vicious cycle. Consequently, our actions (karma) also must be according to thoughts emanating from the mind. It is apt and righteous to deal with the thought process rather than confining to superfluous rituals which are of no consequence. I am least hesitant to say that indulging in meditation can even annihilate past karma because thought and action are vicious as cause and effect one fuelling the other.

I'm given to understand that meditation, trikaranashuddhi (purity and unity of thought, word, and deed), and Bhakti yoga (complete surrender to almighty-being unmindful of results of our deeds) are all fundamentally one and the same and one can lead to other.

The gist of it is…

Meditating just for sake of meditation teaches doing things just for the joy of doing.Being indifferent to thoughts pertaining to the past, or future while in meditation teaches to live in present. Ignoring any kind of thought, be it positive or negative while meditation teaches us not to take success into head or failure to heart, not to succumb to worries, or not to get overwhelmed in happiness.

One greatest boon from meditation is we learn to see things as they are, without opining, judging, or rushing to any conclusion. This development alone is enough to curtail most of our problems due to prejudice. Prejudice plays havoc in our personal, social, and professional domains of life. If we carefully watch all our thoughts, every thought is with reference to 'me' or 'I',and consequently, more selfish is bound to suffer from their thoughts and less selfish are less likely to be troubled by their thoughts. Being selfless doesn't mean foregoing opportunities or being deprived of needs, but not being greedy, avaricious. Surprisingly the more you meditate, the less you worry about yourself, which by itself can facilitate meditation further.More selfish can not be poised and meditation may not be so easily adaptable. In fact, trying to meditate with a motive itself makes meditation a tough task. Meditation by itself silently, unknowingly corrects us, guides us, refines us, makes us realize more of our ignorance, and serves as an unseen teacher, guide, and philosopher.

The influence of meditation on life, its message for the life are so profound. As I said earlier essence of philosophy is all about living in the present and making the best out of it. This is an uphill task as we are constantly vacillating between our thoughts. The only way to dwell in present is by way of meditation. More we meditate more we get to realize what is not, and realize what is life and true values. Relaxation and stress release is trivia, compared to their potential for transforming the personality. Any amount of preaching by any religious preacher, rituals, however intense the prayers are, however arduous the pilgrimage may be, all of them put together even can not bring about the transformation of mentioning worthy. Meditation is a universal approach, transcending all the differences and references, and is all-encompassing. Where it culminates, it terminates all limitations, diversity, and experience of oneness alone remains.

My personal experience with meditation is, not to follow a cult even for meditation, because each cult has its own way of meditation, claiming theirs to be best, and denying others' claims, just like any or every other religion does. This was deeply disappointing for me. When I had my first experience of meditation I was hoping that anyone would do it the same way or teach the same way, but later to my surprise, I came across innumerable cults teaching and practicing meditation in their own way. Not to boast of me, even many of the so-called gurus I met in my spiritual journey, happened to leave me in the lurch. This only has driven me for the search of truth inward, rather than outward, and made me stop seeking a mentor in the world around me. I had a strong conviction that, like the earth is equally close to the root of every tree or plant where it has sprouted from, god must be equally close to every human being, where he has come from. This conviction made me completely rely on myself and I felt happier than ever before. The spiritual journey is an exploration of your own in search of truth. There can't be, need not be a prescribed way to meditate. No one can claim authority. If one claims, he is not authentic...as simple as that.

A laid path can not be exploration

Almighty is ultimate guide

Life is the best philosopher or teacher

Adversity is the best university

And nature, the best parent

Dependency

Dependency is the deadliest of all, particularly psychological dependency. Financial and physical dependency may be momentary. But when it comes to psychological dependency, unless one makes an effort it is hard to break the shell. Overprotected children are more likely to suffer from this even in their adulthood. The priceless blessing a child can have from parents is to learn life skills when parents allow their children to face on their own what they are confronted with and can rise to occasion only when in need.

Anything that makes you feel insecure is ignorance

God-fearing, religious rituals, fear of being punished for wrong deeds are all false spiritual perceptions and I completely antagonize them as they come in the way of spirituality rather. Self-actualization is blunted, the focus is always outwards. Science and spirituality may probably be bridged sometime later in the future through quantum physics and metaphysics somehow or other, but religion and spirituality can never be bridged. Religion is against science while spirituality is beyond science, but not against science. Science and spirituality can even be an extension of one into another but religion, be it any religion, allows only a tubular vision, teaches only perspectives, but never it is open to truth. Religion makes you believe in a set of rules leaving a preconditioned mind that can only accept what is taught to accept and reject anything beyond. Rituals in religion are easier to practice than meditating as they are physical acts and keep us in a false sense of being spiritual.

Meditation asks for mental discipline, taming the wilderness of the mind, and for growth beyond our predilections, passions and emotions, and motives. More we grow spiritually, the more we dissolve difference more universal we become. Our freedom begins not by defining any of our territories, but by not defining territories at all. Religious, political, and geographical differences are arbitrary and manmade and we don't need knowledge of rocket science to realize this simple fact.

I'm of the opinion that it is better to be a rationalist than to be a blind follower of a religion or being a theist. A rationalist rationalizes at least anything that is presented to him. In fact, many rationalists or atheists turn genuinely spiritual and more philosophical than a theist, one who believes in a particular religion or cult. It is beyond comprehension even for a theist to prove the existence of God, or even for an atheist to disprove existence. Both are short-sighted indeed. Particularly religious ideas are borrowed. Believing in one religion and disbelieving in another is all the more foolish. This is like believing in the existence of one branch of a tree and denying other branches, while true spirituality believes and comprehends the root of the tree and can visualize unity in diversity. Most ironic is, there is war among religions to believe in their respective religion for peace!!

Next to spirituality, science is a universal religion, barring its disbelief in spirituality. Religious person disbelieves in other religions, science disbelieves in every religion and spirituality, but spirituality encompasses all religions and even science and beyond. As we progress in meditation we tend to lose self-identity more and more and at one point you become nothing losing that 'I'ness, and feel as though we are merging with cosmic consciousness., or we may have perception of being in everything. It's either becoming nothing or everything …nothing in between. Boundaries disappear, self-identity is lost, and culminates in the perception of oneness. This alone is promising to grow beyond our limitations due to preconditioning of mind and to effectively combat maladies from the individual level to the community level.

Much of our lives are monotonous all through because we carry the past into the present which predetermines the future on the same lines. But with persistent practice of meditation, we gradually delink the past influence, learn to live in present, so that,the path for the future is laid by us with conscious living in present. Reigns of our life, we take completely into our hands, undeterred by influences from the matrix around in which we live.

Our focus on growth and development is always outward. Our mind is both destructive and constructive. Even the science with best intentions proves to be counterproductive sooner or later and it is needless to talk about abuse of scientific knowledgein procuring or making ammunition and overwhelming mechanization eroding human touch gradually in all spheres of life. Even a scientific advancement what is said to be right is proven wrong much later. Drugs designed and accepted today are said to be not so safe and banned much later. More and more automation and sophistication are displacing the human touch gradually in anything and everything. Science never solves a problem without creating many more problems concurrently. Whichever development is against or away from nature, I do not call it development, however scientific advancement you may call it. Such developments are not sustainable.

I'm not against science at all, but our focus is always outward for growth, and the source of all the technology is our intelligence emerging from thinking faculty the mind.The so-called insight we are lacking. It is boundaryless in its thinking and imagination. It can reach the sky or cross the seven seas in a jiffy in its thinking. Power and potentials of the mind are, not explored at all I can say. It's not the intelligence I'm talking about. Its potential in transforming an individual, empowering an individual, and summative changes of all individuals at society and global level, the impact it can have on our depth of thinking have not been realized. The endless health benefits of meditation are testimony of mental power. Barring the knowledge from psychology and psychiatry which only deal with normal and abnormal functioning of the mind, what is known to science and what is explored, or even attempted to explore its potential is negligible only because of prejudice of science towards meditational practices and also because science relies on physical observable parameters for studying anything. Of late of course I see here and there the references relating to meditation in science literature. But certainly, these studies are not adequate and yet to realize infinite possibilities that are possible by unleashing the mental power. Documenting anatomical or physiological changes that meditation can bring about is not an exploration of the mind. Mind is unfathomable for science, be it physical or medical science. Mind is like a bridge between the visible physical world and the vast infinite invisible cosmos. Negligible range of frequencies alone are perceptible to eyes and ears, imperceptible frequencies are incomparable to a perceptible range of frequencies. Our threshold for perception may probably be minimized sensitizing us more for wider and wider perception by the practice of meditation I believe.

Not only perception outward, but we may also even become more sensitive to bodily changes, our nature and depth of thinking and auto regulatory mechanisms in our body must come into play in deeper states of meditation. Though it is out of scope to discuss supernatural powers of mind, I can say with certainty that we have not explored enough and unrealized possibilities can't be denied as such. The most ignored boon to humankind is meditation.

The best part is, it's better learned on one's own than being taught by someone. It makes you more independent. Even on embarking spiritual path, progress on one's own by the inner guide is more progressive than relying on someone as godfather. This is my experience in my spiritual journey because I never relied on a laid path. The spiritual journey is exploration for truth and obviously, a laid path can never be an exploration. This made me believe much more that I had no obligation to go in search of a guru. It is uncovering, unveiling, and discovering of self. Just like in the journey of life one can walk along with you, but no one can walk for you even a guru or godfather at the most can walk along, but it is for you to walk on your own. Self-realization exactly demands the same. Much of life is consumed in our attempts in becoming something. But self-realization needs the experience of being, not becoming.

Meditation is a shift from mindless thoughts to thoughtless mind

Acknowledgments

This is all the will and grace of almighty

I sincerely thank

My brother in law Venkatesan for his immaculate drawings

My daughters Prajnavi and Raghavi for assisting me in editing.

My teacher Dr. Sridhar for penning the foreword in all its glory